CYBERCRIME:
Secure IT or Lose IT

CYBERCRIME:
Secure IT or Lose IT

Denise Marcia Chatam, Ph.D.
Edited by Robert Griffin

iUniverse, Inc.
New York Lincoln Shanghai

CYBERCRIME: Secure IT or Lose IT

iUniverse books may be ordered through booksellers or by contacting:

iUniverse
2021 Pine Lake Road, Suite 100
Lincoln, NE 68512
www.iuniverse.com
1-800-Authors (1-800-288-4677)

Because of the dynamic nature of the Internet, any Web addresses or links contained in this book may have changed since publication and may no longer be valid.

The views expressed in this work are solely those of the author and do not necessarily reflect the views of the publisher, and the publisher hereby disclaims any responsibility for them.

ISBN: 978-0-595-48170-5 (pbk)
ISBN: 978-0-595-60264-3 (ebk)

Printed in the United States of America

This book is dedicated to my children, Charles, Anthony, Crystal, and Marvin; my granddaughter, Arielle; and my parents, who have supported and shared my goals and dreams. Your unconditional support, absolute faith in my abilities, and continuous encouragement made it possible for me to complete this book. A special thank you to Marvin, my youngest son, who became the man of the house and helped in taking care of his niece to allow more time for me to write this book. His patience and maturity were the most critical success factors in my being able to complete the research. Thank you, my children, for all of the personal sacrifices you made over the years in keeping our home together, maintaining your own studies, and keeping your lives in order while I spent countless hours confined to the computer, reviewing literature, and writing. I am eternally grateful for your love and so fortunate to have you in my life. I am truly blessed.

CONTENTS

INTRODUCTION

The United States is the global leader in use of the Internet for commerce and communication. Continued expansion of legitimate Internet use has led to an increase in fraudulent and malicious activities that exploit the Internet, known as cybercrime. Substantial liability accrues to those who ignore cybercrime, and material competitive advantage is available to those who act to mitigate it. Increases in cybercrime attacks and the resulting economic and reputational losses underscore the need to bolster the understanding of the causes and consequences of cybercrime and the need for businesses to comply with information security regulations.

Today, cybercrime is one of the fastest-growing criminal activities in the world. Cybercrimes cover a broad range of illegal activities, including virus attacks, financial scams, downloading pornographic images from the Internet, computer hacking, stalking by e-mail, creating Web sites that promote racial hatred, and defacing business Web sites. Financial cybercrimes include bank, check, debit, and credit card fraud; computer and telecommunication crimes; fraudulent identification, including identity theft; government securities fraud; electronic funds transfer fraud; auction fraud; economic espionage, such as theft of trade secrets; online extortion; international money laundering; intellectual property rights abuses; and work-at-home and online business opportunity schemes. Cybercrimes can cause significant harm, economic and otherwise, to organizations.

Advances in technology have led to increased frequency and complexity of system and data compromises, including compromises of banking and credit card accounts, medical records, student records, and personal electronic communications. Cybercrimes are conducted by a broad range of individuals, from amateur computer users having low-end computers and Internet access in their bedrooms, to organized criminal groups with access to high-end computing resources and skills capable of causing significant harm to businesses and consumers.

Major accounting scandals have also erupted, many facilitated by changes and weaknesses in technology. Because ignorance of the law and illegal activities within an organization are no longer acceptable legal defenses, organizations are now vulnerable to exorbitant legal fees, huge financial penalties, significant damage to their reputation, and even failure of the business.

Publicity about cybercrimes has intensified, primarily because of new privacy and disclosure laws, increased awareness by consumers of the potential for harm, and federal accountability rules and regulations. Regulatory compliance is fast becoming a costly and major liability for all types of businesses. Information security controls are now mandated by the major payment card vendors and banking regulators, affecting all manner of entities, from small retail shops to large corporate financial institutions, from small nonprofit organizations to the largest multinational firms.

Cybercrime is creating large problems for the business community. As reported by government and computer incident agencies, businesses around the world are experiencing continued increases in cybercrime. Businesses in large metropolitan areas in the United States and Europe are ranked at the top in terms of the number of cybercrime incidents. The United States has emerged as a particularly vulnerable population for Internet crime. Organizations of all sizes and from a variety of industries have suffered losses from cybercrimes, although few officially report such incidents. Cybercrimes often yield lucrative financial gains while providing low risks for perpetrators. The level of cybercrime sophistication, automation, and effectiveness is ever increasing.

Gaining a better understanding of the factors that influence cybercrime should assist leaders in the business community, law enforcement, government, and academia in developing programs that minimize cybercrime incidents. Cybercrimes are typically conducted remotely and anonymously to (1) take advantage of flaws in software code, (2) circumvent signature-based tools that commonly identify and prevent known threats, and (3) use social engineering techniques to deceive unsuspecting users into revealing sensitive information or propagating attacks. Various experts, from the FBI to corporate security analysts, warn that as Internet usage grows, e-commerce matures, and intelligence, critical infrastructure, and national defense communities increasingly rely on commercially available information technology, cybercrime will continue to rise.

Cybercrime: Secure IT or Lose IT looks at the who, what, why, when, and where of Internet crime from the perspective of businesspeople. Information security and audit personnel will find value in the materials provided in this book to establish and maintain a comprehensive information security program and to aid in satisfying regulatory compliance requirements.

CHAPTER 1

THE PROBLEM ... CYBERCRIME

You leave the door unguarded to your company's warehouse every day for five minutes during the daily shift change. Would you do something about it? Would you consider a better lock? What about a change to the shifts? Would you consider adding a video camera and motion sensors at the entry? Or would you elect to do nothing because it is only five minutes and there is a cost to make changes? You may consider the risk low because no one will know that you are extremely vulnerable for the 300 seconds. Then the inevitable happens; your business experiences a burglary and loss of property. Due to the loss, you are now willing to overspend to ensure that the unguarded door is never compromised again.

If you shift this thinking toward the Internet, the issue poses a much higher risk. To a hacker, these types of commonplace vulnerabilities represent more than a five-minute open door to a system; they are opportunities to commit harmful cybercrimes anonymously regardless of the time of day or the location of the asset. Hackers capitalize on opportunities every minute of every day, in every country in the world. Although there are numerous law enforcement and government agencies fighting cybercrime around the world, cybercrime remains a lucrative and favored pastime of our youth and a new frontier for organized crime units.

Background

Cybercrime is defined as use of a computer and the Internet to steal a person's identity, sell contraband, stalk a victim, or disrupt operations with malevolent programs. Cybercrime also includes traditional crimes where computing resources are used to enable illicit activity. Cybercrimes include bank, check, debit, and credit card fraud; telecommunications and computer crimes; fraudulent identification, including identity theft, fraudulent government securities, electronic funds transfer fraud, auction fraud, and intellectual property rights abuses; economic espionage, such as theft of trade secrets; online extortion; international money laundering; and work-at-home and online business opportunity schemes. Cybercrime is sometimes referred to as electronic crime, computer crime, high-tech crime, and Internet crime.

Cybercrime is a borderless, global problem that continues to increase as e-commerce matures and use of the Internet grows. Based on countless studies, the United States is the most attacked country and has the largest number of vulnerable machines. The United States is also where most cybercrime attacks originate, with as much as 30% of all attacks coming from that country.[1] With increased computer use in China, a sharp rise in attacks has also been noted in that country. During the last half of 2005, the number of bot-infected computers (a *botnet* is a group of compromised computers using a collection of software robots that run autonomously and automatically in a group of "zombie" computers remotely controlled by "crackers") in China grew 37%. China experienced a 153% increase in attacks, the fastest growth in originating attacks in 2005.

Cybercrime activities can be very expensive for businesses, particularly in countries where enforcement is not as strong as it should be. Many businesses view the tools and processes needed to mitigate the risk of cybercrime as costly *until* they consider the cost of a security breach. The Gartner Group, a research firm in Stamford, Connecticut, estimated that approximately 20% of businesses will experience a serious Internet security problem that is not a virus. Cleanup costs will be higher than the costs of prevention by approximately 50%.

The United States is the global leader in use of the Internet for commerce and communication, and in using electronic commerce for spending. The continued expansion of legitimate Internet use has also led to an increase in fraud that is threatening to exploit the Internet a phenomenon known as cybercrime. Cybercrime poses a risk to both businesses and consumers on a global level. It is a major social issue for business and influences the management of technology and innovation.

The level of sophistication and the effectiveness of cybercrimes are ever increasing. The summer season is the leading hacking season because many would-be computer hackers have extra time because of school and work vacations. Cybercrimes, typically conducted remotely through automation, take advantage of software code flaws, circumvent signature-based tools that commonly identify and prevent known threats, and use social engineering techniques to trick unsuspecting users into revealing sensitive information or propagating attacks. Cybercrime presents a significant risk to the everyday digital activities of consumers and to the digital subsistence of businesses. It is therefore unsurprising that business community leaders and government officials are increasingly concerned about petty criminal acts, organized crime activities, foreign intelligence gathering, terrorism, and other cybercrimes perpetrated by individuals and groups with malicious intent.

Organizations of all sizes and across industries have suffered losses at the hands of cybercriminals although only approximately 9% report such incidents (see Appendix A. Results from the Information Security Survey of the Greater Houston Area). Cybercrimes offer high financial yields and can often be performed in a manner that incurs only modest risks because of the anonymity involved. Lack of incident reporting and ease of storing data electronically have led experts to predict that cybercrime will continue to increase in the years to come. In 2004, the FBI reported that for the first time on a global scale, cybercrime had become more profitable than trafficking drugs.[2]

Japan's National Police Agency reported 1,802 cybercrime cases in the first half of 2006, an 11.8% increase compared to the first half of 2005. Nearly 62% of all phishing scams were aimed at U.S. banks and credit unions, while the number of identity fraud attacks against European and other financial institutions declined. Nearly 40% of non-U.S.-focused attacks were aimed at non-English-speaking countries, with Spain, Germany, and The Netherlands being the primary targets. Germany passed China to become the second-worst country in terms of hosting phishing attacks. More than 14% of all phishing scam e-mails were sent from Germany, followed by China, the United Kingdom, and South Korea. For the second half of 2005, the United States was identified as having the highest percentage (26%) of bot-infected computers, followed by the United Kingdom (22%) and China (9%). Pavan Duggal, a cyberlaw expert in New Delhi, conducted a survey and found for every 500 incidents of cybercrime, only 50—just 1 in 10 were reported. Most of these incidents target individuals; although fewer in number, the most costly incidents occur at businesses.

As reported by AusCERT, the Computer Emergency Response Team for Australia, the most costly cybercrime in 2005 was "denial of service attack," for a total loss of $8.9 million, followed by virus/worm/Trojan horse infections with losses of $2.7 million and computer system abuses with losses of $2.4 million. The estimated loss from computer crimes was $16.9 million as reported by AusCERT. The top 10 countries where complainants and perpetrators resided are illustrated in Figures 1 and 2.

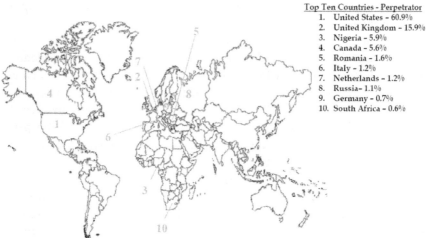

Figure 1. Map. Top 10 Countries by Count: Perpetrators (Number Is Rank)

Note. Adapted from *The IC3 2006 Internet Crime Report. January 1, 2006–December 31, 2006* by the National White Collar Crime Center and the Federal Bureau of Investigation, 2007.

Figure 2. Map. Top 10 Countries by Count: Individual Complainants (Number Is Rank)

Note. Adapted from *The IC3 2006 Internet Crime Report. January 1, 2006–December 31, 2006* by the National White Collar Crime Center and the Federal Bureau of Investigation, 2007.

U.S. businesses are estimated to have lost more than $67 billion to cyber-crime in 2005.[3] This is up from the $14 billion in losses reported in 2004 by the American Insurance Association. Approximately nine out of ten U.S. businesses experienced a cybercrime incident in 2005. The Internet Crime Complaint Center (IC3), a government partnership between the FBI and the National White Collar Crime Center (NW3C), gave an annual report that also suggests that the current trends and patterns of cybercrimes will continue to increase. The research of IC3 indicates that only one in seven incidents of fraud ever captures the attention of enforcement or regulatory agencies.[4]

As displayed in Table 1, in 2006 California was ranked first among all U.S. states in the reported number of cybercrimes. Reports indicate that incidents of cybercrime are also rising more rapidly in the major metropolitan areas of Texas, California, Florida, and New York than the national average.

Table 1

Top 10 Cybercrime States by Count—Individual Complainants and Perpetrators (Number Is Rank)

	Complainants		Perpetrators	
Ranking	State	Percentage of Complainants	State	Percentage of Complainants
1	California	13.5	California	15.2
2	Texas	7.2	New York	9.5
3	Florida	7.1	Florida	9.3
4	New York	5.5	Texas	6.5
5	Pennsylvania	4.0	Illinois	4.5
6	New Jersey	3.6	Pennsylvania	3.3
7	Illinois	3.5	Tennessee	3.2
8	Ohio	3.3	North Carolina	3.1
9	Virginia	3.0	Ohio	3.1
10	Michigan	2.9	New Jersey	3.0

Note. Adapted from *The IC3 2006 Internet Crime Report. January 1, 2006–December 31, 2006* by the National White Collar Crime Center and the Federal Bureau of Investigation, 2007, pp. 10–13.

Many U.S. businesses have been slow in responding with new measures to safeguard their computing systems from intruders. Many company executives fail to see security as adding directly to the profitability of their organization since it is difficult for security experts to prove the losses prevented by improved security and the resulting direct positive impact on profitability. Some businesses have spent millions on a computing security system to make it architecturally sound, only to find that the system fails when a single individual places his or her password on a sheet of paper in an unlocked desk drawer. Cybercrime inflicts more than just economic damage upon a business; it also damages the reputation of an organization, which may require significant effort and cost to repair. Consider the potential impact of a single incident as shown in the following hypothetical situation.

Hypothetical Situation	
A department store database containing the names, Social Security numbers, and addresses of 10,000 customers is compromised by a hacker.	
What is the potential impact?	
Customer notification	$25 x 10,000 = $250,000
Credit monitoring	10,000 accounts x $14/month x 1 year = $168,000 (1 year)
Fraud liability	100 accounts x $1,000 = $100,000
Damaged reputation	*PRICELESS*

The U.S. General Accounting Office (GAO) stated that inquiries by consumers to the TransUnion Credit Bureau's Fraud Victim Assistant Department increased from approximately 35,000 in 1992 to 1.8 million in 2003, a 5,142% increase over 11 years, or an average of a 468% increase annually. In 2005, the Social Security Administration, Office of the Inspector General, received approximately 85,000 allegations of fraud, with 13% (approximately 11,000) involving the misuse of Social Security numbers (SSNs). Of these allegations, 9,500 were converted to open investigations, with approximately 16% involving SSN misuse. These investigations consumed 25% of all investigative resources. From January 2000 to September 2004, the FBI's investigations in the financial institution fraud arena have led to more than 11,466 indictments, 11,362 convictions, and approximately $8.1 billion in restitution orders. According to Javelin Strategy and Research, identity theft resulted in an estimated $49.3 billion lost to U.S. businesses and consumers in 2006.

Several highly recognized surveys have been conducted on cybercrime. The *2001 Computer Security Survey* (Form CS-1), dated July 31, 2002, was a pilot test conducted by the U.S. Department of Justice, Bureau of Justice Statistics (U.S. DOJ-BJS), on cybercrime against businesses. It concluded that there is a need to produce valid national estimates.[5] The Canadian Centre for Justice Statistics conducted a study on cybercrime and concluded that because of ongoing financial losses in the government, law enforcement sector, and business community, there is greater interest in analyzing cybercrime trends. The *Information Security Breaches Survey of 2006* conducted by PricewaterhouseCoopers, indicated there is an ongoing need to help businesses in the United Kingdom and around the globe better understand the risks they face as they embrace the Internet as stated by Alun Michael, the United Kingdom Minister of State for Industry and the Regions.[6] The *Computer Security Institute (CSI) Computer Crime and Security Survey*, a popular but nonscientific study conducted jointly by the FBI and CSI, concluded that there is an ongoing need to promote information protection, increase security awareness, and encourage cooperation between law enforcement and the private sector.[7]

Cybercrimes are complex, typically involving multiple parties in each investigation. Local law enforcement agencies must work with businesses and government agencies that have various organizational structures and sometimes conflicting regulations to follow. Tracing cybercriminals is difficult because the crime frequently transcends a maze of national boundaries and maneuvers through thousands of computing devices and systems.

Cybercrime cases are difficult to investigate because criminals have found complex, technical methods to avoid detection. Hackers are increasingly commandeering vulnerable computers in other countries and using these systems to send spam messages containing programs that can record keystrokes. If a user runs those programs, credit card data and login credentials could be sent back to the hacker, for example. Cybercrime activities have gone beyond PCs and laptops; attacks also target mobile computing and telecommunication devices such as MP3s and IPODs. Audio spam is an emerging security threat in which MP3 audio files are used to send a stock pitch, called a "pump-and-dump" stock scheme. Audio spam avoids filters by using file formats not generally blocked or difficult for filters to disassemble and search. MP3 spam requires a look at bandwidth consumption in transit.

Most law enforcement agencies, because of limited resources, typically do not investigate cybercrimes that are valued at $100 or less. Cybercriminals take advantage of this by expanding the scope of their victimization and money-making opportunities to many victims rather than to just one or two. Most cybercrimes involve more than one victim. When enforcement agencies, such as IC3 investors, can link related complaints and turn them into a $10,000 or $100,000 case with 100 or 1,000 victims, then the crime becomes a more significant matter and law enforcement agencies will invest resources to investigate the crime.

Law enforcement agencies have expressed concerns with respect to the capability of the private sector's and local government agencies' ability to provide protection from cybercrime given the economic impact of the problem. U.S. Secret Service director W. Ralph Basham stated in 2004 that with the potential for cybercrime expanding rapidly throughout the world, the private sector must increase its awareness of cybercrime and become better educated as to its consequences.

To combat cybercrime, organizations will need to become better informed about cybercrime statistics and to share their experiences with cybercrime incidents. By understanding what factors contribute to the likelihood of a cybercrime occurrence, organizations can develop and implement changes that mitigate associated risks and costs. Approaches to cybersecurity will vary, especially among industries and regions where more incidents occur than in industries and regions where occurrences are less frequent and e-commerce is not as widely used.

Problem

Cybercrime has increased dramatically in the United States, soaring, for example, from $14 billion in 2004 to $67 billion in 2005, a 480% increase in just one year. This level of increase is repeated in other countries around the world. Nine out of ten businesses are affected by cybercrime, yet less than 10% report an incident to law enforcement or government agencies tracking these crimes.[8] Since 2002, the number of cybercrime incidents recorded by government and computer incident agencies continues to rise, as do their sophistication and complexity. The increase in cybercrime attacks and the resulting economic and intangible losses underscore the need to bolster understanding of the causes and consequences of cybercrime.

The United States and countries around the world are becoming increasingly dependent on cyberspace for their military, commercial, and social interactions. At the same time, the vast and ever-expanding interconnected electronic networks are under constant attack, and a country's ability to defend them or to counterattack is weakened by a lack of coordination and policy constraints within the country and internationally. In order for the developed world to maintain its leadership, these countries must also maintain cybersuperiority. The vulnerability of that capability has been demonstrated repeatedly, such as in an attack by hackers in the United States in June 2006 that shut down some of the Pentagon's unclassified computer systems and disrupted the e-mail system in the secretary of defense's office. This was one of the more significant of the thousands of attacks annually against military computer and Web networks. In the United Kingdom,

Germany, and other countries around the world, the same types of attacks against the military have been reported.

Cybercrimes ignore geographical boundaries. For example, because of lack of a special "chip-and-pin" technology in the United States, fraud involving credit cards in the United Kingdom increased by 126% in the first half of 2007. In the United Kingdom, credit and debit cards have a microchip that helps to authenticate a personal identification number (PIN) during purchases and cash-machine withdrawals. If a card lacks the microchip, banks will not permit the transaction. In the United States, fraudsters can copy the magnetic stripe on the back of a card and steal a person's PIN simply by attaching "skimmers" to a cash machine or by using small cameras recording the PIN the person enters. According to the Association of Payment Clearing Services, in 2006, U.S.-based fraud using cards from the United Kingdom totaled $34 million, overtaking France as the number one place to convert United Kingdom credit and debit card details into cash.[9]

Businesses are vulnerable to coordinated attacks that could yield credit card information of thousands of customers or steal valuable blueprints on new products. Nations are vulnerable to coordinated attacks that could destroy the entire electrical infrastructure of large geographic areas for months, according to the U.S. Department of Energy.[10] The vulnerability is compounded by the fact that equipment used by business is often manufactured in countries other than the one in which it is deployed and databases of customer information are maintained offshore by third party providers with less stringent regulations, granting potential access to criminals to the equipment and supporting computing resources, including software programs and passwords. Increasingly, businesses are beginning to take the warnings seriously, yet too often still fail to provide the funds necessary to prevent these types of potential catastrophes.

Theoretical Explanations of Cybercrime

Willie Sutton, a notorious American bank robber from the 1920s to the 1950s, was once asked why he repeatedly robbed banks. He said, "Because that's where the money is." The theory that crime follows opportunity is a time-honored maxim in criminology; opportunity reduction is one of the pillars of crime prevention.

Cybercrime is a social issue involving technology, innovation, and criminal management. Theoretical explanations of cybercrime include the *differential association, rational choice,* and *crime prevention theories.* Edwin H. Sutherland's differential association theory states that a criminal act occurs when a situation is appropriate for the person who plans to commit the act. It also posits that crime is prevalent in all classes of society lower, middle, and upper classes. Sutherland summarizes by stating that a theory of crime must explain both common and white-collar crime. According to Sutherland, industry and size define the classes of society. For example, a multinational technology organization would be at the upper end of society classes. An individual providing cleaning service would be at the lower end of society classes. The differential association theory states that crime is prevalent for all classes and wherever opportunity exists for it to occur. The theory also states that the potential impact lessens when reducing the opportunity of cybercrime, for example, by applying sufficient resources to prevent it, is the focus of an organization.

The rational choice theory, originated by the 1700's criminology pioneers and utilitarian philosophers Cesare Beccaria and Jeremy Bentham, states that humans are reasoning actors who weigh means and ends, costs and benefits, and make a rational choice based on these factors. The theory describes crime as an event that occurs when a perpetrator elects to risk breaking the law after considering his or her own need for money, personal values, learning experiences, how well a target is protected, how affluent the targeted neighborhood is, or how efficient the local police are.

Ronald Clarke's crime prevention theory focuses on reducing crime opportunities rather than on the characteristics of criminals or potential criminals. The foundational strategy of the theory is to reduce the rewards of committing a crime by increasing the associated risks and difficulties. The crime prevention theory states that patterns in criminal activity are based on location and reflect a concentration of opportunities for crime called *hot spots*. Like the rational choice theory, the crime prevention theory defines the opportunity.

Historical Perspective

The abacus, originating circa 3500 B.C. in Asia, is considered one of the earliest forms of a computer. In 1820, a textile manufacturer in France named Joseph-Marie Jacquard created the loom, which allowed repetitive weaving of fabrics. Jacquard's loom was another precursor to the modern-day computer. The new technology caused Jacquard's employees to fear that their livelihoods would cease to exist. To discourage use of the loom, the employees committed acts of sabotage, the first recorded instance of computer crime.

Cybercrime has been in existence since data have been stored in electronic form. Individuals and teams representing all socioeconomic, gender, age, racial, and national groups commit cybercrimes. Early forms of cybercrime included identity theft used by fugitives to avoid capture, check forgeries, and negotiation of stolen or counterfeit checks. The new generation of cybercriminals has proliferated, with cybercrime growing rapidly and in complexity. Advances in computing technology such as digital color printing, multimedia applications, and the Internet have enabled amateurs to produce high-quality counterfeit documents.

Four major factors contribute to cybercrime:

1. It is easy to learn.

2. Few resources are required compared to the potential harm caused.

3. It can be committed remotely.

4. Many "cyber-offenses" are not clearly illegal.

Massive databases of learning institutions, financial institutions, and airline companies that store credit card and other identification

Figure 3. Edwin H. Sutherland, Criminologist

information for legitimate purposes are also used at greater frequency to launch cybercrimes that are more complex and broader in scope. These factors are major contributors in making cybercrime one of the fastest-growing crimes both in the United States and worldwide.

In 1949 criminologist Edwin H. Sutherland, pictured in Figure 3 coined the term *white-collar crime* in his book entitled *White Collar Crime*.[11] Sutherland's *white-collar criminality theory* states that white-collar crime is a major nonviolent crime and leads to financial costs that are usually several times as large as the financial cost of all the other crimes that are customarily regarded as larger financial crime problems. Cybercrime is largely a white-collar crime.

When Sutherland introduced the concept of white-collar crime, he had in mind a successful white male, middle-class professional. He assumed that white-collar crime was crime committed by offenders who have a high social status and respectability, determined by their professional duties. He thought that criminal behavior was a learned behavior rather than primarily a pathological or biological behavior. This sentiment became the basis for his differential association theory. Sutherland noted that (remember, this was 1949) females were less likely to commit crimes because they are destined to bear children and are more closely supervised than males. He also asserted that traits of masculinity such as aggression, competition, rationality, machismo, and power were contributors to criminal behavior, unlike feminine characteristics such as sweetness, sensitivity, irrationality, and obedience.

Donald Cressey, a leading expert in organized and white-collar crime in the United States and a student of Sutherland's, studied the *repression of crime theory.* He stated that if strict controls were imposed on all personnel within a business, then violations such as embezzlement, fraud, and other violations would be greatly reduced, but very little business would be done.[12]

Criminologist Marshall Clinard compared places with little crime, such as Switzerland, with places having a great deal, such as the United States. Reviewing corporate crime and corrupt practices in the United States, his goal was to answer the question of whether the maintenance of moral boundaries through the identification and punishment of crime is necessary for societies characterized by relatively low crime. Clinard found that it is the attitude of society toward crime that makes the difference. He found that populations with training in civic virtue, even though citizens may be armed, do not experience sensational massacres or high crime rates. This model of citizenry is how Switzerland is defined. The United States also allows its citizenry to be armed, and the majority of citizens live peacefully, yet some subcultures do not.[13]

Marshall Clinard and Peter Yeager defined corporate crime as "any act committed by corporations that is punishable by the state under administrative, civil, or criminal law."[14] They suggested that white-collar crimes are sociological as well as legalistic and that such behaviors may be unethical or immoral in the corporate context but not explicitly violate any laws. For example, an information security analyst who cheats on his security reports by altering the results may not have violated a law or regulation but may instead have violated an ethical rule or norm of the information security community. The act of altering security reports is a white-collar offense because the information security analyst has engaged in an unethical or immoral behavior within his occupational context.

The primary types of cybercrimes are data, network, access, and other crimes. Cybercrimes falling under the category of data crimes include data interception, data modification, and data theft. Data interception is the interception of data in transmission. Data modification is the alteration, destruction, or erasure of data. Data theft is the taking or copying of data in violation of laws protecting data, such as copyright and privacy laws, the Health Insurance Portability and Accountability Act, and the Gramm-Leach-Bliley Act.

Cybercrimes against computer networks include network interference and network sabotage. Network interference is impeding or preventing access by others. The most common example of network interference is a distributed denial of service (DDoS) attack, which floods an Internet service provider (ISP) or a Web site.

DDoS attacks use many hacked computers that follow the commands of the perpetrator. Changes to or destruction of network systems is called *network sabotage*. Network sabotage frequently occurs with ghost accounts, accounts that are not closed when an employee leaves a company and can give a disgruntled employee a backdoor into the network.

Access crimes include unauthorized access and virus dissemination. *Unauthorized access* is the hacking or destruction of a network or system. For example, the U.S. DOJ reported on March 1, 2006, that a federal computer security specialist within the Department of Education's Office of Inspector General installed software on the computer of a supervisor, enabling him to access its stored data at will. He later used this privileged access to view e-mail and other electronic transactions of his supervisor, then shared the information with others in his office. The accused pled guilty and was later sentenced to five years in prison and fined $250,000.[15]

Virus dissemination is the introduction of software that is harmful to a system or data therein. In 2005, the U.S. DOJ reported that a twenty-one year-old man of Beaverton, Oregon, used more than 20,000 infected computers he had infected with a computer worm program to launch a DDoS attack against eBay in 2003. The attack caused a denial of service for legitimate users who wanted to access eBay. The perpetrator, still awaiting sentencing, could receive up to ten years' imprisonment, a $250,000 fine or twice the gross gain or loss, and three years supervised release.[16]

Other types of cybercrimes include aiding and abetting cybercrimes and computer-related forgery and fraud. *Computer-related forgery* is the alternation of data with the intent to represent it as authentic. *Computer-related fraud* is the alteration of data with the intent to gain economic benefit from its misrepresentation. In February 2006, the U.S. DOJ reported that a 41-year-old man of Cleveland, Ohio, obtained stolen debit card account numbers, PINs, and personal identifier information of the true account holders and encoded the data on blank cards. He used the counterfeit debit cards to obtain $384,000 in cash advances from ATMs in the greater Cleveland area over a three-week period. The perpetrator received a sentenced of 32 months in prison, three years of supervised release for bank fraud and conspiracy, and was ordered to pay $300,749 in restitution to the bank and $200 to the Crime Victims' Fund.

Personal and financial information is at the core of business transaction records and that identify customer information. The volume and value of personal and financial information make it very attractive to those with criminal intentions. Federal, state, and local legislation as well as the marketplace regulate governance of the information. Keeping sensitive information away from those with malicious intent is a growing problem for all. Legislation exist encouraging and requiring law enforcement personnel and business leaders to do more in protecting sensitive information, and still fighting cybercrime remains a major issue.

Primary reporting agencies tracking cybercrime incidents find that such incidents are underrepresented for businesses and consumers due to the low level of cybercrime incident reporting and the difficulty in detecting and punishing the crime. Many victims elect not to report a cybercrime incident because they think reporting the crime is not worth the effort. Despite the reluctance to report, the number of crimes against businesses and consumers reveals a rapid increase in cybercrime activities, and the associated costs are staggering. Joschka Fischer, the foreign minister of Germany, stated that the global costs were more than $40 billion a year in 2006, and that this is only the beginning. This figure includes cybercrimes of far-right extremists, terrorists, and peddlers of child pornography as well as data espionage, data theft, and credit card fraud.[17]

CHAPTER 2

CYBERCRIMINALS AND THE LAW

Cybercrime is big business and is growing in reach, complexity, and level of harm experienced by its victims. The cybercriminal of yesterday was focused more on self-gain. The cybercriminal of tomorrow will be focused more on causing harm to large segments of the world's population through electronic warfare and compromising key infrastructures. Knowing this, now what?

Reporting Agencies

White-collar crime is considered a specialist field of study within criminology, a field historically shunned by many criminologists as well as governments and the private sector. Student criminologists of white-collar crime have a difficult time because they are met with distrust and suspicion on the part of those they study. Criminologists must be careful in suggesting direct and conscious links between management and harm because they can lead to libel charges. Management is how leadership runs an operation at the time of an incident. Harm is the consequences experienced by a business form an incident. Some experts assert that some white-collar criminals act like members of subcultural groups in defining their illegal behaviors as acceptable.

Most countries have a primary law enforcement agency that investigates cybercrimes, with local and regional law enforcement agencies serving as the agency where a complainant begins the reporting process. In the United Kingdom, the Serious Organized Crime Agency is the primary enforcement agency, whereas in the United States the FBI is the primary agency. The FBI considers cybercrime its third priority given the increasing pervasiveness and costs associated with it. The importance given to fighting cybercrime is exceeded only by that placed on protecting the United States from terrorism and foreign counterintelligence operations and espionage.

Below is a list of primary reporting agencies for countries with the greatest number of reported cybercrime incidents. Most countries are members of Interpol, which is responsible for investigating transnational crimes. Canada, France, Germany, Italy, Japan, Russia, the United Kingdom, and the United States are members of the G8 Subgroup on High-Tech Crime, a group that works to combat cybercrime and enhance cybercrime investigations.

Table 1. Primary Reporting Agencies

Country	Primary Reporting Agency
Argentina	Policía Federal Argentina
Australia	One police force for each of the six states and the Northern Territory, and the Australian Federal Police
Brazil	Departamento de Polícia Federal (DPF)
Canada*	Royal Canadian Mounted Police (RCMP)
China	Ministry of Public Security
France*	Police force under the authority of the Minister of the Interior
Germany*	State Ministry of the Interior, Federal Crime Investigation Police
Greece	Ministry of Public Security
India	Central Bureau of Investigation (CBI)
Italy*	State Police (Polizia di Stato), the Carabinieri, and the Finance Guard (Guardia di Finanza)
Japan*	National Police Agency (NPA)
Mexico	Ministerial Police and the Federal Preventive Police [Policía Federal Preventiva] (PFP)
Netherlands	The National Criminal Intelligence Service (Centrale Recherche Informatiedienst or CRI)
Nigeria	Nigerian Police
Romania	Regional Center for Combating Transborder Crime
Russia*	Militia, the Ministry of Internal Affairs
Singapore	Singapore Police Force
South Africa	South African Police (SAP)
United Kingdom*	The Serious Organised Crime Agency (SOCA)
United States*	Federal Bureau of Investigation (FBI)

NOTE: * denotes a member of the G8 Subgroup on High-Tech Crime Member, a group that works to combat cybercrime and enhance cybercrime investigations.

The U.S. Cyber Initiative and Resource Fusion Unit (CIRFU), a spin-off from IC3, was created to help eliminate false leads and refine cases before they are referred to a local or international law enforcement agency or task force. CIRFU is supported by major targets of cybercriminals—online organizations and merchants like Microsoft, eBay and PayPal, and industry trade associations like the Business Software Alliance, the Direct Marketing Association, the Merchant Risk Council, the Financial Services Industry, and others.

Investigation

In addition to the FBI, many other governmental agencies conduct their own investigations in the United States, such as the U.S. Securities and Exchange Commission. The same is true of other countries around the world where multiple agencies also conduct their own investigations. In October 2007, the SEC announced that "Operation Spamalot" was effective and led to a 30% decrease in financial spam and a 50% cut in spam-related complaints. The initiative targeted the issuers of mass e-mails that preyed on novice investors urging them to buy the stock of a touted company. The messages would claim the touted stock had a bargain price and was poised for a steep increase. The perpetrators would then sell the stock if the price was hiked by naïve investors believing the information in the spam emails. Below is an example of bogus stock advice sent via e-mail.

Subject:	This is where it's at!
Date:	Sun, 14 Oct 2007
PPYH Stirs Investors As More Properties Are Being Acquired. PHYSICAL PROPERTY INC (PPYH) Price: $ 0.25 The list is growing and Vision City has been identified as next for acquisition. More news is expected on Monday. Review the Website and read the news. Give your broker a call, and tell him to move on it.	

Part of any investigation is gathering data for evidence. When the crime is a cybercrime, a method for obtaining stored electronic data from the source is needed. Although laws exist for giving law enforcement a method to compel providers to disclose the evidence, the actual implementation of these laws varies. The United States and Australia have laws that authorize the collection of this type of evidence with distinctions between the disclosure of the content of communications and data related to such communications. In the United States, a subpoena is needed to access provider information and a search warrant to search a home or business to obtain data from computers. In Australia, police officers must have a court order to compel the disclosure of the traffic information but not for the disclosure of communications' content. Conversely, in the Philippines and Japan, providers are permitted to disclose stored data upon request from a police officer; however, if the provider refuses, a search warrant is required.

Once the data have been gathered (availability), preservation (integrity) and confidentiality are critical to an investigation and future use of the data for prosecution, penalty assessment, and taking corrective action. In Taipei, Taiwan, law enforcement must pay large sums of money to reimburse providers for the disclosure of data. In the United States, however, providers are entitled to "reasonable" costs. Most governments do not pay anything for these disclosures. Data preservation is just as important as data gathering in order to preserve the evidence. In Australia and the United States, law enforcement may request preservation without judicial oversight. Japan and Indonesia have a less formal process. In Taipei, providers are required not to disclose the fact that law enforcement has made a request. In the United States, the law precludes providers from notifying their customers without a court order. In Japan, providers face criminal prosecution if they interfere with a criminal investigation by notifying customers.

Cyberforensics

Cyberforensics is the practice of extracting data and information from computer storage media and ensuring their reliability and accuracy. Conducting any type of cyberforensics involves the challenges of electronic evidence discovery, collection and data preservation, and evidence presentation using an approach acceptable in a court of law. Electronic evidence can easily be modified and is fragile. Cyberforensic investigations are conducted with the investigator working under the assumption that cybercriminals are dishonest, and even if perceived to be honest, will still hide, disguise, wipe, encrypt, or destroy evidence from storage media using shareware, freeware, and commercially available utility programs.

Cyberforensics is both an art and a science, and remains in its infancy. As technology evolves and mutates and revolutionary changes occur, the rules central to cyberforensics also apply to the fields of auditing, security, and law enforcement, which must also change or risk becoming obsolete and ineffectual. This necessity is leading cybercriminals to new methods and better means for perpetrating their crimes.

An investigation begins with the investigator's determining what computer or computer systems are affected. Next, if possible, the investigator will take a quick picture of the screen to document that the computer was running and what was running at the time, and the investigator pulls the power plug from the back of the computer, rather than the outlet, to reduce further loss of evidence. By pulling the power plug from the back of the computer, changes due to power are stopped instantly. Pulling the power plug from the wall gives a second more of power to the unit that can alter the state of the computer. Next, the investigator will tape or use other material to cover any open disk drives and CD/DVD drives, and begin recording pictures and videotaping basic information about the computer. This would include the computer make, model, serial number, any attachments to the computer such as routers or speakers, and the state of the machine. The investigator will create a forensic image of the computer or computing system, and then save the image in read-only mode. Once saved, a copy of the same image is opened. The next step is to search through the image looking for key words or files, possibly over a specific period that have been accessed, modified, or deleted. This process can yield all kinds of information, from credit card numbers and passwords to hidden files and deleted files.

The next step is to open the computer and take more pictures or video capture the number of hard drives, any peripherals connected such as network and sound cards, and the condition of the computer. All parts are labeled, tagged, and bagged, and the computer is taken to a crime lab for further investigation. Before leaving, the investigator scans the area around the computer, including wastebaskets, for any documentation, such as sticky or handwritten notes with passwords that may also contribute to the investigation. Each tag has the date and time collected, name of the investigation, where collected, and any other pertinent information regarding the item. The computer and its parts are placed in an appropriate container for transport, confiscation of the source computer is handled by law enforcement, and the evidence is stored in a secure place. Taking these extra measures, although tedious and time-consuming, these steps will help to ensure the integrity of evidence, enable investigators to develop a stronger case, and allow for use of the evidence in a court of law.

Cybercriminals and Other Troublemakers

Comparing crimes committed in the physical and virtual worlds can unveil some of the anonymity of those who perpetrate cybercrimes. Marcus Rogers, Purdue University professor of cyberforensics research, has defined cybercriminal types as shown in Table 2.

Table 2. Cybercriminal Taxonomy. Types of Cybercriminals by Skill Level and Motivation

Newbies, Novices, and Aggressive Young Criminals, or Script Kiddies
• Limited computer and programming skills
• Rely on toolkits to conduct their attacks
• Can cause extensive damage to systems because they do not understand how the attack works
• Looking for media attention
Cyberpunks and Middle Market Criminals
• Capable of writing their own software
• Have an understanding of the systems they are attacking
• Many engaged in credit card number theft and telecommunications fraud
• Have a tendency to brag about their exploits
Internals **(can become any type of cybercriminal; the most dangerous and least understood)**
a) Disgruntled employees or ex-employees
• May be involved in technology-related jobs
• Aided by privileges they have or had as part of their job function
• Pose largest security problem
b) Petty thieves
• Include employees, contractors, consultants
• Computer literate
• Opportunistic take advantage of poor internal security
• Motivated by greed or necessity to pay off other habits, such as drugs or gambling
Coders
• Act as mentors to the newbies; write the scripts and automated tools that others use
• Motivated by a sense of power and prestige
• Dangerous have hidden agendas, use Trojan horses
Old Guard Hackers
• Appear to have no criminal intent
• Alarming disrespect for personal property
• Appear to be interested in the intellectual endeavor

Organized Crime, Malicious Companies, and Professional Criminals
•   Specialize in corporate espionage
•   Guns for hire
•   Highly motivated, highly trained, have access to state-of-the-art equipment
Information Warriors/Cyberterrorists
•   Increase in activity since the fall of many Eastern bloc intelligence agencies
•   Well funded
•   Mix political rhetoric with criminal activity; political activists
•   Possible emerging category
•   Engage in hacking

Source: [Adapted from Ann Bednarz and Marcus Rogers, "One Man's Hacker Taxonomy." http://computerworld.com (accessed October 14, 2007). Used with permission.]"

Four primary cybercriminal groups are shown in Figure 4. The skill levels and motivations outlined in Table 2 further define these groups. First are organized crime gangs that use data obtained maliciously for money laundering, extortion, child pornography, and human trafficking. These groups present a high probability of harm at increased frequency. Second are malicious companies that install and use spyware to gather user information without the user's knowledge; still other organizations use adware to send unwanted advertisements. The adware and spyware programs are often resident on a machine without the knowledge of the user. Malicious companies present a high probability of harm at low frequency. Middle market criminals who steal and sell data to third parties and engage in other criminal activity constitute a third cybercriminal group. Middle market criminals present a low probability of harm yet the frequency of an occurrence is high. Middle market criminals are known for creating botnets, networks of compromised computers giving an attacker control. Comprising the fourth group are amateurs, novices, aggressive young criminals who exploit data to create counterfeit documents to gain services under a fictitious name, such as altering driver's licenses, medical record cards, or student grades. This type of cybercriminal is also known to be mischievous. Novice, aggressive young criminals present both a low probability of harm and a low frequency of an occurrence.

**Economic and Noneconomic Harm and Frequency
Of Occurrence Based on Type of Cybercriminal**

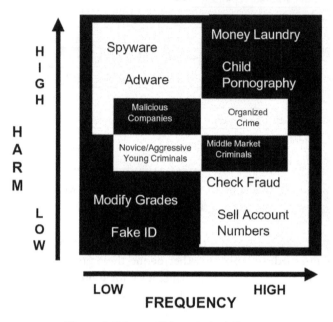

Figure 4. Primary Cybercriminal Groups

Attackers rent botnets to spammers or other criminals such as organized crime groups and script kiddies. Script kiddies are amateur hackers who use existing and easy-to-find programs, techniques, or scripts to find and exploit weaknesses on other "Internet-attacked" computers. Script kiddies conduct random searches and have little regard or understanding of the potential harm. Today, botnets are the moving force behind online organized crime, giving criminals opportunities with low risks and high profits. For example, in 2006, organized crime groups earned approximately $2 billion in the United States from phishing scams.[18] These scams involve victims being tricked into disclosing financial and other personal information. In 2006, Symantec indicated that the use of botnets is decreasing, yet where they persist, botnets are being used more aggressively for sending spam or new attacks. Much of the decline can be attributed to the increase in e-mail filters, antivirus programs, and personal firewalls.

The original hacker stereotype was that of a smart, lonely deviant, a young male who is computer savvy and has poor social skills. As with most stereotypes, it may apply to only a few individuals. Some computer criminals are techie mavericks that enjoy writing and releasing destructive code such as viruses. Others are white-collar professionals who steal copies of their employer's customer databases to use elsewhere or disgruntled employees with the intent of launching an attack on their employer. Some are con artists intending to defraud consumers by stealing their personal information and using it for financial gain or to acquire services fraudulently. Business leaders, information security personnel, law enforcement, and consumers should learn more about the personality traits, skills, and methods used by cybercriminals.

Patient cybercriminals have been able to gradually remove IT security obstacles and have matured beyond DDoS attacks to cybercrimes causing even greater dollar losses. The more people know, the more they can all help in pursuing cybercriminals. As with any criminal, understanding what motivates cybercriminals to get involved in computer crimes, how they select targets, and why they continue the deviant behavior is crucial to combating cybercrime.

Motivations vary among cybercriminals and include money, revenge, curiosity, and ego. The novice cybercriminal using prewritten scripts is driven by the thrill of an attack, experimentation, or media attention. On the other end of the spectrum are the professional criminals motivated by financial gain or the desire to cause serious harm to a business, government, or society, preferring to remain anonymous and not seeking media attention or ego satisfaction. This means that businesses must do more than rely on technology; they must also become knowledgeable about the motivation and mind-set of cybercriminals to mitigate computer security risks.

Persons who begin by first learning to use computers and then move to hacking are usually motivated by curiosity or ego. Conversely, those who begin with criminal thoughts or tendencies and then learn to use computers are usually motivated by money or revenge, and to a lesser degree ego. Those motivated by curiosity or ego create various levels of destruction. Script kiddies take advantage of a weakness within an operating system. Exploiting this weakness determines the level of destruction. Many who seek revenge are company insiders or recently released disgruntled employees who target intellectual capital such as supplier and customer databases, product prototypes, business plans, and leads. These individuals typically have more access, understand how systems operate, and know where to strike.

Cybercriminals who seek to make money do not want to kill the host; rather, their focus is to get in and out without being detected. Those seeking revenge tend to be the most dangerous and the most destructive. In the 1990s, the primary driver for cybercriminals was to see how systems were configured and what damage they could cause to a system. Today, the biggest driver is money, a big change in the stereotypical hacker image of a young male introvert driven by loneliness and social awkwardness and sitting alone in his bedroom with a computer consuming all of his free time.

Cybercriminals have an advantage over those who investigate cybercrimes in that hackers readily share information with their peers to help one another through a problem that may impede the completion of a cybercrime. For example, a hacker is unable to access a router or get through a firewall. The hacker will post his or her dilemma on the Internet through various channels looking for assistance. Those within the hacking community will assist the hacker in completing his or her hack. The same type of information sharing among businesses, victims, and investigative resources does not occur. Victims are reluctant to report cybercrimes, businesses share only enough information to limit liabilities, and governmental agencies have inconsistent methods of gathering and tracking data on cybercrime activities, all of which together leaves little hope for sharing. This leads to weak, reactive mode of operation for victims, businesses, and law enforcement, rather than a proactive position of strength.

Organized criminals in areas such as Eastern Europe and in the Asia-Pacific regions are, at increasing levels, penetrating business systems and threatening organizations with the release of sensitive data unless they are paid money. Such online extortion typically goes unreported, because most businesses do not want to discuss the incident or share any details for fear that it may encourage others to attempt the same or expose the company to liability and cause harm to shareholder value. The Internet Crime Complaint Center (IC3) estimated that in 2006 approximately 10% of these incidents were reported. A major reason is that extortion is difficult to document and prove. Another method of extortion is to launch DoS attacks that interrupt a company's electronic operations, and then advise the company that the DoS attacks will stop when the extortion money is paid.

Cybercrime is so attractive because the number of cybercriminals successfully captured and brought to trial is low. Even fewer are prosecuted. By some estimates, as few as one out of four hundred are caught. For those who are captured, tried, and convicted, the monetary penalty may be small, jail time, if any, may be minimal, and the crime is often classified as a misdemeanor. The small percentage of cybercrimes garnering attention are typically those perpetrated by the novice, less-skilled deviants, who distract attention from the many organized crime gangs and malicious companies with dangerous and highly skilled criminals operating around the world.

Convicted identity thieves, for example, have about a 50% change of avoiding jail time, based on a study reviewing closed U.S. Secret Service case files by Utica College, IBM, and the FBI in 2007.[19] Perpetrators who were convicted and imprisoned typically served sentences of three years or less. Printers, mobile phones, and computers were used in about half of the cases, and for ID thief, the Internet was the exclusive tool of choice 10% of the time. The median loss from identity theft was approximately $31,000. There was one incident where the losses totaled approximately $13 million.[20] In general, victims experienced higher losses when more perpetrators were involved in a case.

Much of the investigative resources are spent on the novice user sitting in his basement running the latest worm attack, the low end of the spectrum, rather than organized crime groups that can launch terrorist attacks or conduct economic espionage, the dark side of information warfare and the high end of the spectrum.

Cyberspace today gives cybercriminals the advantage, contributing to the attraction of committing these crimes. The advantages include the following:

1. asymmetrical payloads (performing an action when triggered) and starting ratios

2. anonymity or invisibility of attacker to the target

3. zero warning or latency

4. swift strike advantage

5. fluidity of attack mode

6. ability to vary the frequency and intensity of an attack

7. multiplier effects available to the attacker

8. scalability easily achieved

9. target placed in reactive mode

10. target required to contain collateral damage

11. target's behaviors forcibly changed, and

12. ethical and legal ambiguities.

Five World-Famous Hackers

Willie Sutton, a notorious American bank robber from the 1920s to the 1950s, was once asked why he repeatedly robbed banks. He said, "Because that's where the money is." The theory that crime follows opportunity is a time-honored maxim in criminology; opportunity reduction is one of the pillars of crime prevention.

Four famous cybercriminals, Vladimir Levin, Johan Helsingius, Kevin Mitnick, and Robert Morris, and Leo Kuvavev, who have captured global attention.[21] Vladimir Levin, a St. Petersburg (Russia) Tekhologichesky University math graduate, was the mastermind of the Russian hacker gang that broke into Citibank's computers, getting $10 million. Levin used his AO Saturn office computer, a St. Petersburg, Russia computer organization. He was arrested at London's Heathrow Airport in 1995.

Johan Helsingius was the creator of the popular remailer program penet.fi. This program functioned on a standard 486 having a 200-megabyte hard drive. Helsingius never tried to remain anonymous, one of his trademarks. After abandoning the remailer, Helsingius' home was raided by the Finnish police in 1995 based on complaints received from the Church of Scientology. The church claimed that a penet.fi customer had posted secrets of the church on the Internet.

Kevin Mitnick, also known as Condor on the Internet, sent messages to his friends on computers in a Radio Shack store using the *Internet Relay Chat* (IRC). IRC is a form of Internet chatting or conferencing. As a teenager, Mitnick could not afford his own computer and would use the demonstration computer models on display to dial into other computers. He was convicted and sentenced to one year in a residential treatment center and classified a computer addict. Mitnick later became the first hacker on an FBI "most wanted" poster, and became known as the "Lost Boy of Cyberspace" because of his repeated offenses.

Robert Morris, son of the chief scientist of the National Computer Security Center, U.S. National Security Agency, was known on the Internet as "rtm." He graduated from Cornell University. His father, who brought home a computer from work, introduced him to computers. Morris was labeled a star user at Bell Labs, where he held an account because of his earlier forays into hacking. He later became known for the 1988 Internet worm he unleashed that significantly damaged the early Internet and infected or crashed thousands of computers. His hacking activities became common knowledge, resulting in widespread use of the term *hacker* by businesses, consumers, academia, and law enforcement.

Leo Kuvayev, known as BadCow, is a Russian-American spammer, considered to be the ringleader of one of the world's largest spam gangs. He and six partners were fined $37 million as a result of a lawsuit by the Massachusetts attorney general. Kuvayev was found to be responsible for millions of unsolicited e-mails per day and performed a DDoS against BlueSecurity Company. He has also registered hundreds of domains through various registrars in China, France, and New Zealand to illegally sell software, drugs, and more.

These cybercriminals became technically savvy with time and practice. Their starting point began with experimentation. Over time, each gained criminal expertise, with the crimes increasing in complexity, reach, and level of damage. All caused significant harm to their victims yet received little in the form of punishment for their actions. If ego and notoriety were motivations for their criminal actions, then they succeeded. Typical of many cybercrimes, the harm is not always financial or economic; rather, the intangibles or noneconomic damages caused the greatest harm, such as the posting of secrets.

Cybercrime Today

Major Cybercrimes of Record

Major cybercrimes of record have mainly involved criminal intrusions into computer networks, systems, and databases. Many case studies from countries like Japan, New Zealand, and Romania have found that cybercrime knows no borders, yet the reporting of these crimes does. Table 3 is a snapshot of major cybercrimes that have occurred over the last twenty years.

Table 3. Major Cybercrimes of Record, 1986–2007

Major Cybercrimes of Record 1986–2007	
1986	The Hanover Hackers and Legion of Doom
1988	**Internet Worm.** Robert Morris, $196m losses, Internet stopped; took three days to eradicate
1995	**Mitnick.** Government alleges $80m losses, source code changes
01/1999	**"Cyber warfare."** Civil rights abuses ignite LoU, 2 Chinese hackers sentenced to death
04/1999	**Melissa Virus.** $300m, David Smith imprisoned (PC Explore.Zip)
12/1999	**Credit Card Fraud.** CD Universe, 300,000 cards, blackmail threat of $300,000
02/2000	**DDoS.** E-commerce attack, Yankee Group, ~ $1.2b losses; Yahoo/Amazon/Ebay/CNN/Buy.com
05/2000	**ILoveYou** Worm (vbs.loveletter.a). ~ $1.0b losses in the Pacific Rim, Europe, and North America
08/2000	**Barclays Bank.** Security breach revealed 1000's of individual banking accounts
07/2001	**Code Red + Variants.** $1.2b globally (Nimda, Korna ++)
2004	**DDoS.** Attack against London's Online Gambling Sites; Russian Organized Crime Today, Cyber Terrorists Tomorrow; The Year of the BOT (and BOT Nets)

Major Cybercrimes of Record 1986–2007	
2005	**Zobot and Mytob Worms.** Attacked computers globally, including ABC, CNN, the New York Times, and Daimler Chrysler by repeatedly shutting down and rebooting computers; tied to a war between rival virus writers.
2006	**Cell phone batteries depleted** by repeatedly awakening an idle phone, sapping its electric power; new types of attacks emerging; unprecedented spike in junk e-mail (spam) and sophisticated online attacks from increasingly organized cybercriminals due to the increased number of security holes in widely used software
2007	**Estonia, European Union cyberattacks on private and government Internet sites** after a decision to move a Soviet-era statue from a square in Tallinn provoked outrage from some Russian nationals in Estonia. **TJX Cos** security breach, theft of personal data, affected 94 million accounts 65 million Visa and 29 million MasterCard numbers.

Cybercrime Trends

The following is a list of cybercrime related trends:

- Big businesses are gaining confidence while small businesses are becoming less secure.

- Businesses are pressured by cybercrime and insider abuse in parallel with increasing and evolving compliance demands.

- Cyberattacks are increasingly being launched on weekdays during standard U.S. working hours of 9 to 5, suggesting that online crime is evolving into a full-time profession for many.

- Microsoft Internet Explorer remains the most frequently targeted Web browser.

- The summer season is the primary season for hacking because many would-be computer hackers have spare time because of work and school vacations.

- The United States is the target of most DDoS attacks.

- Botnets are getting larger.

    o   China is the country with the highest number of bot-infected computers.

    o   Beijing is the city with the most bot-infected computers.

    o   The United States had the highest percentage of bot command-and-control servers.

o At any given time, between three and four million bots are active on the Internet.

o Symantec reports a 7% increase in botnet-infected computers in 2007.

o The average command and control center is up and running for only four days.[22]

- There is a significant increase in the number of software security vulnerabilities uncovered by researchers and actively exploited by criminals. For example, Microsoft issued ninety-seven fixes for security holes in 2007, including fourteen critical flaws known as zero day threats. This is up from thirty-seven in 2005.

- Click fraud, those that generate bogus commissions for affiliates and those that target a competitor's ads to burn up the competition's advertising budget, are leading to class action lawsuits against Internet powerhouses such as Google and Yahoo.

- Company character assassination spam is emerging as a new threat.

- Criminals are getting more sophisticated at evading any anti-cybercrime efforts, such as using the same Web servers for Web sites that target multiple banks and e-commerce companies, and routing traffic to those servers through home computers that they have commandeered with bot programs.

- Criminals are going from trying to hit as many machines as possible to developing techniques that allow them to remain undetected on infected machines longer.

- Criminals from the United States and Poland in increasing numbers are selling credit card, bank account, and identity theft information on the Internet.

- Home users are being targeted more than businesses.

- Keyloggers and spyware infecting devices are more prevalent than easily detected viruses and worms.

- Malware, spyware, viruses, and worms continue to cause major headaches for everyone, including businesses, government agencies, and ordinary tech users.

- Most breaches occur because information was not properly protected.

- New Trojan horse programs are being introduced that morph themselves each time they are installed on a computer in order to evade antivirus software.

- Nigeria has the largest number of perpetrators of phishing attacks using get-rich-quick schemes, using the names of fictitious dignitaries and family members and asking an unsuspecting victim to share in the deposit of funds.

- Stock tips and inexpensive medicines are among the fastest-growing form of spam.

- Temporary, disgruntled, or terminated employees commit the majority of all fraud and data theft.

- The most common source of data leaks are lost or stolen laptops, personal digital assistants (PDAs), and memory sticks/thumb drives. This is followed by records lost by third-party business partners, misplaced or stolen backup files, and use of malware programs.

- The number of hackers targeting utilities increased by 90% in 2007, to an average of ninety-three attacks per utility per day.

- The number of phishing attacks is increasing.[23]

- The United States ranked as the top country of attack origin in 2006 and 2007.

- The greatest threats to information security are computer-assisted fraud, industrial espionage, sabotage, employees, hacking, and vandalism.[24, 25]

Cybercrime Incident Reporting

Over the last twenty-five years, the growth in the power and sophistication of computer systems has increased our dependence on these systems. The trend in the near term is upward acceleration in the use of these systems. The vulnerability of an organization to an attack grows as its dependence on computing resources increases. In 1998, it was reported by the FBI that approximately 17% of cybercrimes were reported to government authorities; in 2003 it was noted by the FBI that 50% of all attacks were reported, an increase of 33% over a five-year period. Based on many studies, the number of cybercrime incidents reported is decreasing rather than increasing, with many citing only 10% of incidents as being reported. According to one study, 22% of businesses did not know if their Web site had experienced an unauthorized access. Another study reported that as many as 83% of businesses have experienced some form of cybercrime. The real number of cybercrime incidents remains unknown; the true severity of cyber-crime is under-represented.

The IC3 is the recommended location to report an incident of cybercrime. IC3 does not provide information on a specific cybercrime incident nor does it provide data on a local basis to the public. These data restrictions limit the capability to conduct secondary analysis of IC3 data, particularly at a local level. Many businesses and consumers are not aware that incidents can be reported to this agency.

Cybercrime incident reporting varies widely among businesses and consumers. Many businesses report a computer security breach to law enforcement only when mandated by law or the severity of a computer security breach is significant enough to bring potential harm to the business' reputation or to a large segment of their customers. Multiple perspectives exist on when and under what circumstances a business should report a computer security breach. In the State of California, for example, Senate Bill (SB) 1386 states that a business is required to give, within 48 hours, notice of a discovery of a security breach to a law enforcement agency. Conversely, in the State of Texas a business is encouraged to notify law enforcement.

The trend in cybercrime incident reporting suggests an increase in the number of incidents reported each year. Businesses do not report incidents for many reasons. The two prevailing reasons are the need for the business to protect consumer confidence and the desire to retain shareholder value. Other factors include changing federal, state, and local policies; technological advancements that are making it easier to commit cybercrimes; not knowing whom to contact; or the feeling by victims that nothing is gained or worth pursuing by reporting a cybercrime incident. Many cybercrime incidents are never reported because the victim simply did not consider reporting the crime.

Legal and Ethical Issues

A computer security breach is by law ambiguous. The law states that a computer security breach is the unauthorized acquisition of computerized data that compromises the security, confidentiality, or integrity of personal information maintained by an individual or business entity.[26] A computer security breach occurs, for example, when an outside hacker gains unauthorized access to a system or when an employee obtains personal information from an employer's computer system that is not required to perform his or her duties. This is an example of a computer security breach vulnerability within a computer system that becomes a cybercrime.

As cybercrime affects more lives, nations will struggle to establish a common understanding and agree upon international conventions for regulating conduct in cyberspace. This struggle ranges from first-strike policy during warfare to the frustration of extraditing or prosecuting individuals from a country different from the country where the cybercrime incident occurs. For example, U.S. authorities were unable to pursue hackers from Switzerland who attacked the San Diego Supercomputing Center because of "dual criminality." A lack of common conventions exists. Multilateral codes and conventions to address the characteristics and ramifications of strategic information warfare are needed. The Internet creates the ability to perpetrate cybercrimes in indefinable or undiscoverable geographic space such that no courts could convincingly claim jurisdiction. Where laws are deficient in an area of cybercrime within a country, that country could operate as a haven for groups and individuals for that specific type of cybercrime. For example, a country lacking Internet laws on defamation could become a haven for groups or individuals who maliciously commit such acts.

Responding to cybercrimes effectively requires cooperation within and between countries in a timely manner. The ability for law enforcement to cooperate in transborder investigations requires definite legal authorities. This lack of cooperation is used by cybercriminals to their advantage; they often choose to commit crimes against victims located solely in other countries. Without the ability of each country to prosecute these domestic offenders or extradite them to the country where the victims reside, that country can become a safe house for the criminal activity. To close the gap, some countries, such as Malaysia and the United States, have enacted laws that allow them to prosecute domestic offenders for harm caused to foreign victims.

Funding and adequate resources are significant problems in developing a cybercrime investigative unit. Countries have developed various models to address apprehension and prosecution of cybercriminals. The United States, Japan, and Canada, for example, employ a task force model, in which resources from several law enforcement agencies are pooled together. The task force model distributes the funding burden across each agency and the model leads to a more viable cybercrime unit.

An alternative approach used by many countries is the development of a cybercrime investigative capacity at the national level that is available to assist investigators at the regional or local level, where fewer resources and experience exist. Malaysia, the Philippines, Japan, and Canada have law enforcement institutions at the national level that serve this function.

The hiring and retention of qualified investigators is difficult. Hong Kong and China, for example, elect to hire cybercrime investigators only from within the police force and provide them with training in computer technology. Conversely, the United States typically seeks to hire individuals who have computer expertise and provide them with training in investigative skills. Japan, Hong Kong, and China have strict policies of rotating police employees to different assignments, and with this rotation their cybercrime experts are moved into other jobs. Other countries, such as the Philippines and the United States, lose their experienced investigators to the private sector as security consultants because they can make more money. Administrators for cybercrime units have sought ways to limit the rotation of their experienced investigators and to provide both monetary and nonmonetary incentives for investigators to continue working at the law enforcement agency.

There is value in having cybercrime investigators work with prosecutors in pursuing an investigation. Hong Kong, China, and the United States have asserted that U.S. prosecutors have played a valuable role in such investigations by focusing on the evidence required to be successful at trial. Thailand and some other countries have legal systems that do not allow prosecutors to become involved in investigations.

The Intelligence Authorization Act requires the president of the United States to submit annually to Congress updated information on the threat to U.S. industry from foreign economic intelligence collection and industrial espionage. The PATRIOT Act expands the authority of U.S. law enforcement to help in fighting terrorism and to detect and prosecute other crimes such as cybercrime used to support terrorism. The Health Insurance Portability and Accountability Act (HIPAA) provides regulations for use by healthcare providers, their vendors, and those who have access to sensitive data to safeguard personal health information on every individual. The Gramm-Leach-Bliley Act (GLBA), also known as the Financial Services Modernization Act of 1999, provides limited privacy protections against the sale of an individual's private financial information and codifies protections against pretexting, the practice of obtaining personal information through false pretenses. The Payment Card Industry (PCI) standards provides for the integrity, availability, and confidentiality of account information for all who have access to this sensitive data for as long as the data storage is required.

In 2004, the southern African country of Zambia passed tough legislation that would give convicted computer hackers and other offenders fifteen- to twenty-five-year jail sentences. This law is known as the Computer Misuse and Crimes law. A young computer expert who accessed the State House Web site and replaced the picture of then president Frederick Chiluba with a cartoon committed the offense that instigated the legislation. He was arrested and charged with defaming the head of state, but the case was dropped since at the time there were no provisions in Zambian law to deal with cybercrimes.

Many consumers and business leaders are looking to government to do more, while others have stated that citizens are surrendering too much in the name of security that is temporary at best. For example, in Europe, the use of a national identification card is commonplace; however, there continues a great debate over its use in the United States. One of the greatest benefits cited by the government is that a single database will contain information on all citizens within a country, as is the case in the United Kingdom, whereas today each state and territory in the United States has its own system, one that is proprietary and partially integrated, at best. Privacy rights advocates have stated that the migration toward a single database could lead to less personalization and control of our private information. Conversely, the U.S. government states that implementation of a national ID card could be used to better fight terrorism because all law enforcement agencies would have access to the same information. They support this argument with one of the findings published by the 9/11 Commission, which stated that a contributor to the failure in communications was that each agency had pieces of information on some of the attackers, but none had information on all of the known attackers. With a centralized database, a federal law enforcement agency such as the Federal Bureau of Investigation (FBI), the Immigration and Naturalization Service (INS), or the Central Intelligence Agency (CIA) would have potentially had access to information on all attackers that could have resulted in a greater opportunity of apprehension prior to the event.

CHAPTER 3

CYBERCRIME UP CLOSE: THREATS, VULNERABILITIES AND EXPLOITS

Since it will come, be it by e-mail, or by the unsuspected Web page that wants us to run 'that' program ... be aware now rather than later.

Cybercrime threats are on the increase. Drug lords prey on the more vulnerable layers of modern society. Cybercriminals get their income by stealing from middle-class working people. The current waves of attacks are designed to steal data for profit without causing damage to systems. Hackers are migrating from large attacks to targeting computers and Web applications to steal confidential information. On the horizon are cyberattacks targeting critical infrastructure such as electrical power grids for days at a time across a region and disruption of air traffic by intercepting, shutting down, or rerouting telecommunications traffic for hours. The common denominator of most crimes is usually that victims lack security awareness, lack security measures, or both. This lack of awareness can lead to various types of losses. Businesses and consumers should learn to expect an attack and not be surprised when it comes.

Cybercrime gains a foothold from targets not having countermeasures in place, leading to vulnerabilities ripe for exploiting. These risks or threats are what a threat agent will exploit to cause exposure to loss of money, productivity, time, or reputation.

Threats

A *threat* is an unwanted, dangerous action that may result in harm to an asset that is otherwise in good working order. For example, if an organization has antivirus software loaded onto its computer system but fails to keep it updated, then that organization is now vulnerable to virus attacks. This unwanted action could be deliberate or accidental. Threats come from within an organization, such as from a disgruntled employee, or externally through a dissatisfied customer or a hacker looking randomly for a target. The degree of a threat depends on the skills, knowledge, resources, authority, and motives of the attacker.

The two distinct categories of cyberthreats are (1) national security concerns as Internet technology matures (cybertheft of sensitive data, cyberterrorism, and foreign-based computer intrusions) and (2) the host of possible threats, such as theft of intellectual property, online sexual exploitation of children, and Internet fraud with any computing device having Internet access.

The basic instruments used by perpetrators are cyberattacks, illicit file sharing, intrusions, and illegal use of cybertools. Terrorist organizations, foreign intelligence agents, and criminal enterprises have increased their use of encryption technology to secure communications so that they can command and control operations and people without fear of surveillance.

Employees and human errors or failures are the most common type of threat. These are acts conducted with no malicious intent. In most instances, lack of training and experience or false assumptions and overlooked situations lead to this type of threat. Employees have frequent access to data within an organization. Mistakes made by employees can easily lead to revealing sensitive data, storage of data in unsecured areas, the input of erroneous data, the accidental changes or deletion of data, and other forms of failure to protect information. Most of these threats are preventable through controls and enforcement.

Hackers often use well-known exploits targeting specific businesses. For example, in 2003 there was a targeted threat aimed at financial institutions called the *BugBear B*. This virus became increasingly harmful upon the specificity of the target. If antivirus software active on the system did not remove the virus from the infected system, the virus would delete all data on the system. This virus would wait for employees' keystrokes that revealed usernames and passwords on connected systems. Once the sensitive information was collected, the virus would forward the data to any of ten e-mail addresses stored within the virus.

Hackers are often stereotyped as young males having limited parental supervision and spending all of their free time on a computer. This stereotype has been broken, with hackers ranging in age from ten to sixty-five, being male or female, and having various backgrounds and technological skills that are internal or external to an organization. Hackers are classified as either *script kiddies* or *expert hackers*. Script kiddies have limited skills and use others' software to conduct their crimes. Expert hackers develop software scripts and code exploits and share them with others. Hackers are also known as *"crackers"* and *"phreakers"*. Crackers are those who crack or remove protection designed to prevent unauthorized duplication, and phreakers are those who hack the public telephone network.

Other examples of threats are those faced by the 2008 U.S. presidential candidates. These candidates face phishing threats that involve attacks that harvest credit card numbers or divert online contributions to an opponent's campaign, creating high risk to the Web operations of the 2008 presidential candidates. The candidates' campaign Web sites are prime targets for phishers who can create bogus sites posing as the legitimate site to harvest contributors' credit card and bank account numbers. The candidates can also become victims of their opponent's radical followers. The diversion of donations under these conditions has the potential to undermine confidence in the online donation concept because phishers are more capable and candidates more dependent on the Internet.

Phishers are becoming better organized and have expanded their craft from the Windows-based system to Linux, which is considered more secure than Windows. The Linux operating system is typically highly reliable and good for running server software. Because Linux machines can be used to easily create specially crafted networking packets, they can be used in highly sophisticated online attacks. As attackers learn how to exploit this capability of compromising Linux machines, the machines are becoming highly coveted by online attackers, who can receive a premium in the underground market for compromised machines.

Computer viruses and worms are software programs that mimic life forms, known as a type of cyberplague. *Worms* are programs that propagate over a computer network from one computer to another by breaking into the computers in the same fashion hackers breach computers. An emerging threat to PC nets is the "superworm," which some believe is controlled by Leo Kuvayev, the notorious fugitive spammer. An example of a superworm is "Storm." The creators of the Storm worm botnet used a multiphase process that evolves over time to deploy this malware through botnets. The malware is named Storm because of the storm-related subject lines its infectious e-mails use, such as "250 dead as storm hits Cancun" or "Australians shoot down a U.S. missile." The initial phase began in 2006 by infecting Windows machines but not causing much harm. This worm continues to gather strength by infecting more Windows machines in preparation for the second phase. This worm was considered the most successful of the new breed of worms in 2007.

The Storm botnet has become powerful enough to force interruption of entire economies of the Internet and is estimated to potentially execute more instructions per second than some top supercomputers. This botnet consumes a great deal of bandwidth, a concern for security administrations and analysts. The worm is written by hackers seeking profit, not fame, and is unstoppable today. Antivirus programs have been unsuccessful in blocking it. The full impact remains unknown because symptoms of infection do not appear quickly and infected computers can sit dormant for extended periods. This has made eradication of the superworm difficult for antivirus companies.

A more sophisticated technique of propagating cybercrime is the *fast-flux service network*, a growing threat on the Internet. Fast-flux service networks are networks of compromised computer systems with public *domain name server* (DNS) records that constantly change as frequently as every few minutes. DNS is an Internet server or service that translates *Internet protocol* (IP) addresses into domain names. These constantly changing architectures make it more difficult to trace criminal activities and shut down their operations. The purpose of fast-flux is to render the IP-based block list, a popular tool for identifying malicious systems, useless for preventing attacks. (An *IP* is an identifier for a computer or device on a *transmission control protocol/Internet protocol* [TCP/IP] network, similar to a telephone number as an identifier for a physical address.) The research on fast-flux is new and remains a mystery for researchers and Internet service providers (ISPs).

Information Warfare Threats

Information warfare (IW) is a growing form of cybercrime that has become a major intelligence challenge on the battlefield, in managing geopolitical conflicts, and in managing critical infrastructure supporting computing systems. Advances in IW have outpaced the typical user's understanding of the concept. IW is about information dominance over an adversary by learning where force can be most productively applied against a target, while preventing the target from learning the attacker's critical points. IW attacks leave systems vulnerable to exploitation, penetration, and degradation. The intensity of these actions increases as an economy's dependence on such networks increases. The potential uses of these measures can includes warfare, economic crises, international competition, and criminal activities. Unlike other forms of cybercrime, IW is governed by a strategy focused on an objective. The objective may be military, political, economic, or some combination of the three. IW also involves developing techniques and capabilities.[27]

IW operations target or exploit a specific information resource to increase the data's value to the offensive player while decreasing its value to the defensive player. Cyberwarfare creates a winner and a loser, and it involves nonconsensual or hostile acts. The offensive player seeks financial gain, thrills, amusement, credentials to participate or join, or wants an advantage over or revenge against the victim. For the victim, the stakes may include loss of life, privacy, productivity, public confidence, and competitive position; fines and penalties; and other financial losses. Cyberwarfare may also include crippling critical infrastructures such as air traffic, electrical power, or telecommunications and interruption of military communications.

Regardless of the ultimate objective, IW attacks begin with an information system that is typically an electronic system. That system, the initial attack target, becomes victim to receiver overload, data corruption, computer shutdown, or data erasure, for example. This attack is known as the *technical attack method.* A technical attack can also be used to degrade or negate other elements of an IW operation. Other technical effects include signal blockage and system paralysis on information systems, causing delayed or wrong decisions. Communication intrusions and network worms also cause delays, confusion, and deliberate shutdown of unaffected nodes, and can lead to wrong decisions.

IW requires support from external sources so that the attacker knows the locations of communication nodes, access protocols, addresses, login IDs, and passwords, for example. The perpetrator must also learn how a target system contributes to the adversary's situation, and what information the system can provide to help the cause. The same knowledge is needed to affect the decision process and criteria used by the adversary to know whether to block, degrade, falsify, or insert certain information. Sensors for monitoring and electronic intercept, access points and tools for computer network analysis and probing, and reconnaissance to detect and locate notes must support IW. IW requires resources that are considered experts and possess an understanding of the target and the scenario of interest in order to develop an effective IW strategy.

Table 4. Information Warfare Topology, Threat Level and Offensives

Offensive Information Warfare Threat Typology		
Level 1	Destroy tangible information assets	Seeks to destroy computer systems and data networks through the use of brute force, or denying information or access to these systems.
Level 2	Achieve denial of service	Seeks to prevent the selected target from operating effectively, ranging from irritating acts to defacement of a Web site.
Level 3	Degrade information systems content	Seeks to degrade or corrupt content on a target system such as using malicious software (malware) or a network worm.
Level 4	Infiltrate information systems	Seeks to infiltrate a system or resource in order to conduct espionage and pass or publish concealed information; does not entail destruction.

Offensive Information Warfare Threat Typology		
Level 5	Engage in perception management	Entails silent penetration of a target system to shape opinions or foster deception to play mind games such as inserting false information. Seeks to be silent and invisible.

Source: Adapted from Cronin, Blaise, and Crawford, Holly. 1999. Information Warfare: Its Application in Military and Civilian Contexts. http://www.indiana.edu/~tisj/readers/full-text/15-4%20cronin.pdf (accessed October 21, 2007) [used with permission].

IW attacks on computers and networks typically launch a single attack that generates multiple effects on numerous targets by combining some or all of the approaches defined in Table 5 based on the desired level of threats.[28] Other forms of IW attacks use a combination of approaches for an explicit objective, such as data denial, cover and deception, data insertion, and attacks on communications and computer systems.

Organized Crime Threat

Organized crime groups are drawn to the easy money and low risks associated with crimes conducted in cyberspace. Organized crime gangs who use the Internet for fraudulent activities are a significant and growing threat in cyberspace. Usually, one or more components of the Internet are used for conducting fraudulent transactions, fraudulent solicitations to prospective victims, or transmitting proceeds of fraud to financial institutions or others connected with the scheme. The threat from organized crime is global, with many schemes originating in Eastern Europe, China, and the United States. Organized criminals have begun to collaborate, with clearly defined roles. Execution of crimes is conducted like a business plan, with the capital investment to support the initiative. It is expected that the mob will begin to work together in collaboration with hackers to form a more organized cybercrime community over the upcoming years. Organized crime has made huge advancements in cybercrime, creating a new class of smarter criminals to lead.

An example of the advancing skills of organized crime groups is Lexitrans, an Overland Park, Kansas, company. Senior leaders of the business were indicted on federal charges after allegedly operating a shell company to market adult Web sites and 900 numbers. These sites advertised free trials yet charged users. Investigators stated that the illegal operation generated $750 million in revenue, the largest consumer fraud in the United States as of 2007. This crime was linked to the famous Gambino crime family. There was a data center in Overland Park of approximately 7,000 square feet with redundant power and fiber-optic pipes. Lexitrans was paying $100,000 daily for placement of its ads on popular search engines and $50,000 per month for Internet access.[29] This was not an isolated incident. The implications are far-reaching, including risks to national security and to Web hosting operations that do not want to be linked publicly to a U.S. Homeland Security-related crime.

Threats to Information Assets

The objectives of information threats include gathering trophies, general mischief, financial gain, warfare, revenge, and protest. The major security requirements of a system for overcoming threats to information assets are availability, integrity, and confidentiality as defined by ISO/IEC 27001, Clauses 3.2 through 3.8. ISO (International Organization for Standardization) and IEC (the International Electrotechnical Commission) collectively form the specialized system for worldwide standardization for managing information security. This international standard provides guidelines and the general principles for initiating, implementing, maintaining, and improving information security management within an organization. Availability (Clause 3.2) is defined as ensuring that authorized users have access to information and associated assets when needed. Confidentiality (Clause 3.3) is defined as ensuring that information is accessible only to those authorized to have access, and integrity (Clause 3.8) is defined as safeguarding the accuracy and completeness of information and process methods. This approach serves as the foundation of most information security methodologies and regulations in place today, such as Sarbanes-Oxley (SOX) and Basel II. Major threats affecting information assets are shown in Table 5.

Table 5. Types of Threats to Information Assets

Types of Threats to Information Assets		
AVAILABILITY	**INTEGRITY**	**CONFIDENTIALITY**
Destruction	Alteration	Penetration
Degradation	Falsification	Espionage
Malware, Virus, and Other Attacks	Superimposition	Misappropriation

Availability

Availability is the requirement that an asset be accessible to authorized individuals, entities, or devices. Critical components typically have higher availability needs. An interruption in service could indicate the inability for end users to access computing resources when needed. Loss of availability could translate into productivity, financial, and customer losses. Types of threats that can interrupt availability include destruction, degradation of data and systems, and malware that can make data inaccessible.

Destruction and Degradation

Forces of nature, known as *forces majeure* or "acts of God," include earthquakes, hurricanes, fires, and lightning. They are dangerous not only because of their inherent destructive power but also because they come unexpectedly, not allowing adequate time to prepare. Such threats can disrupt the lives of individuals and business operations, including the storage, transmission, and use of information.

Technical hardware failures or errors can occur because of a cyberattack or through flawed equipment distributed by a manufacturer. The defects that result from either of these occurrences can result in unstable services, lack of availability, or other unexpected system issues. Terminal or unrecoverable losses of equipment can occur from some errors. Intermittent errors leading to faults that are difficult to repeat may also manifest.

Other forms of destruction and degradation include technical software failures or errors that can occur because of purchasing or acquiring software with undisclosed faults. Computer code written and sold by both trusted and unproved sources may contain unrevealed or unresolved bugs. As software is loaded, compatibility issues may arise, resulting in the unique combinations of some hardware and software exposing new bugs. These new bugs may not be errors but rather programming leftover shortcuts for honest or dishonest reasons. This has led to the common practice of announcement of upcoming patches and offering free patches for software available for download from the Web site of vendors.

Malware and Other Attacks

Software deliberately designed to attack a system is known as *malware*. Malware damages, denies, or destroys services to the target system. Macro and boot viruses, Trojan horses, backdoors and trapdoors, DoS attacks, worms, polymorphs, and hoaxes are all forms of malware.

A *macro virus* is a virus that is encoded as a macro placed within a document. Nearly three-fourths of all viruses today are macro viruses. Once a macro virus is on a computer where the target application resides, such as Microsoft Word or Excel, it can embed itself in all future documents created by the application. A *boot virus* loads when a computer is started and the operating system is launched. A *worm* is a unique virus type that can replicate itself and uses memory but does not attach itself to other programs.

Trojan horses, also known as logic bombs, are an IW tool used to gain access to information. Trojan horses are a form of masquerading. A *software Trojan horse* is a program that executes an undesirable action not anticipated by the individual executing the program. *Time bombs*, a type of Trojan horse, activate on a specific day as designed in the code, such as with the Friday the 13th or April Fool's Day Trojans.

A *backdoor* is a way to access a computer system, network resource, or application that bypasses security mechanisms. A backdoor may be installed to grant access for troubleshooting or other purposes. Attackers use detected backdoors or install themselves as a function of an exploit. Worms can take advantage of a backdoor created by an earlier attack. For example, Code Red left a backdoor for the complex virus Nimda to enter. Nimda infected files, performed mass mailings, modified existing Web sites, and propagated LANs by spreading itself in attachments named README.EXE in September 2001. Backdoors are security risks exploited by crackers who are always looking for any vulnerability to exploit.

A DoS attack uses multiple compromised systems to attack a single target by sending a large number of connection or information requests to the target. The flood of bogus and legitimate requests for service causes a denial of service for users on the targeted system. A system crash or an inability to perform ordinary functions could result. DoS attacks on a single compromised system could generate new attacks on other systems, or a *distributed denial-of-service* (DDoS) attack. A DDoS attack begins with a hacker taking advantage of vulnerability in one computer system and making this system the DDoS master. A DDoS attack is a coordinated flow of requests released against a target from many locations simultaneously. From the master system, the intruder communicates with other systems that can be compromised. The intruder then loads hacking tools on multiple compromised systems, even thousands of them. Using a single command, the intruder directs the controlled machines to launch the flood of attacks against the specified target. In a mail-bombing attack, the attacker routes large numbers of e-mails to the target.

Two major DDoS attacks, known as DNS Backbone DDoS attacks, occurred in October 2002 and February 2007. These attacks each lasted a few hours, disabling nine of the thirteen DNS root servers on the Internet backbone. These attacks translated text-based Internet host names into IP addresses, disabling the Internet itself rather than specific Web sites. These attacks are believed to have originated in South Korea.

Polymorphic code is code that mutates while keeping the original algorithm intact. An *algorithm* is a formula or set of steps for solving a specific problem. As part of a virus, polymorphic code mutates and replicates, deceiving scanners looking for fixed patterns. The first-known such virus, a semipolymorphic virus called "1260," was written in 1990 by Mark Washburn. It was later followed by the first real polymorphic engine, called the Mutation Engine (MtE), written by Dark Avenger, a hacker from Bulgaria.

IP scans and attacks on compromised systems are attacks by hackers who scan a random IP address or a range of local IP addresses and targets for known vulnerabilities, sometimes from earlier exploits. IP scans and sweeps are a common form of active reconnaissance scans that ping an Internet control message protocol (ICMP) for DoS amplification attacks, a simple network management protocol (SNMP), and other protocols to identify existence of machines. ICMP supports packets containing control, error, and informational messages. SNMP is a set of protocols for managing complex networks. Passive reconnaissance scans that are hard to detect, such as eavesdropping on wireless LAN (wardriving), are also prevalent.

Other types of attacks include Web browsing, unprotected shares, mass mailings, SNMP vulnerabilities, spam, and hoaxes. Web browsing attacks are infected systems having write access to a Web page and infecting Web content files. When users browse these pages, their system becomes infected. Unprotected shares are used to copy viral component to all reachable locations on a file share. E-mail infections are spread via mass e-mailings to addresses in address books. Spam, unsolicited commercial e-mail that is a nuisance, is emerging as malware and viruses to propagate attacks. SNMP vulnerabilities compromise and infect network monitoring systems. A *hoax*, the transmission of a virus hoax with a real virus attached, is a devious approach to attacking computer systems.

Viruses

In 1983, Fred Cohen wrote the first virus to demonstrate security holes. According to Cohen, a virus is a program that can infect other programs by modifying them to include a possibly evolved version of itself. A virus is a fragment of code that attaches to other computer instructions such as macro instructions within documents, software application code, or code for booting a computer.

Virus-infected systems contaminate specific common executable or script files on all computers the virus can attach to. Viruses are usually unstoppable, even by the authors themselves, and typically cause logical, not physical, damage to a system. The two functions of a virus are cloning itself and dispensing a payload. During cloning and while running, the virus will add its code to existing files so that the new code will run along with the code that was infected.

There are three types of cloning viruses—file infectors, boot infectors, and multipartite viruses. *File infector viruses* attack executable files, such as macros in Excel documents. *Boot infector viruses* infect the boot sector of disks; some also use concealment techniques such as stealth, encrypting, and polymorphic code. *Multipartite viruses* infect both files and the boot sector of systems. Viruses focused on concealment include stealth, encrypting, and polymorphic viruses. *Stealth viruses* capture system calls and then return false information. *Encrypting viruses* conceal their presence by storing their code in an encrypted format. *Polymorphic viruses* mutate and replicate from scanners looking for fixed patterns.

When the virus delivers its payload, the virus triggers an action. The trigger may deliver its payload when the payload is activated or may wait until a trigger is activated (such as a specific date or the number of times a file has been executed). The actions triggered can delete files, stop computers from starting, swap characters on screen, and clone themselves to fill a disk, display messages, or crash machines.

Viruses are sometimes mistakenly call computer worms and Trojan horses. A virus must be attached to other computer instructions as part of a host to cause harm. Conversely, a worm can spread itself to other computers without needing to be transferred as part of a host. A Trojan horse is a stand-alone file that appears harmless until executed. A common method to initiate entry is through e-mail or accessing an infected Web page.

Integrity

Integrity has two primary properties that make it more difficult to characterize than availability and confidentiality. The first property is the idea that the data stored for an asset should be trusted. The second property is that there is an expectation that appropriate people will modify an asset in appropriate ways. For example, a bank customer's account information is stored in a database security. The bank teller must trust that the account information is current and accurate. Second, if data are damaged or inappropriately altered by a user, the data should be restored to a trustworthy state with little or no loss. Using the bank account example, assume the bank teller, who is authorized to view and update customer account information, is angry with his employer and wants to sabotage a customer's account to make the bank look bad. The customer's account information is an example of an asset that has a high rating in terms of integrity. Inaccurate account information could cause the customer to become exposed to theft, experience serious financial harm, incur financial losses, be subjected to litigation, or suffer a damaged reputation.

Alteration

Alteration of computer data includes the modification, variation, partial change, erasure, or input of data, or suppression of computer data or programs, corresponding to the falsification of a legitimate document. Alteration is considered a form of computer fraud and can be considered computer forgery if the offense as prescribed by law constitutes forgery when committed intentionally and without right. Categories of computer alterations include assumption of false identity in e-mail messages for fraudulent purposes, use of bogus Web sites that falsely present themselves as the sites of established organizations for fraudulent purposes, posting false information on Internet bulletin boards to manipulate stock market prices, creating templates for making false identifications on a Web site available to others (such as driver's licenses), and making electronic price tag alterations where online retailers are the victims. *Data diddling*, another form of alteration, is an attack involving the changing of raw data before it is processed by a computer then changing it back after the processing is completed.

Currently a new debate is emerging in which ISPs are attempting new measures to manage traffic on their networks. The U.S. cable network provider Comcast has begun impersonating users and resetting connections to control peer-to-peer (P2P) traffic on its network. This is in an effort to maintain quality of service. Comcast will cut off uploads of files to P2P networks by injecting TCP resets that are forged as coming from a customer. This is an issue for some because they consider Comcast to be impersonating customers. Comcast, an ISP, must be in a position to manage its traffic because of the amount of outbound and inbound traffic in its network. As the amount of outbound traffic increases, inbound rates decrease. This requires Comcast to throttle outbound P2P traffic to maintain service quality for inbound traffic. To many, this is comparable to a telephone operator breaking into a telephone conversation, impersonating one of the speakers, saying, "It is time to go now, goodbye," and closing the connection.

Computer records can be altered easily. Opposing parties to a lawsuit sometimes allege that computer records lack authenticity because they may have been tampered with or changed after they were created. In one such case involving computer records and the federal rules of evidence, *U.S. v. Whitaker*, 127 F.3d 595, 602, 7th Cir. 1997, the government retrieved data from the computer of a narcotics dealer named Frost.[30] The data from the computer included detailed records of narcotics sales for three aliases: "Me" (Frost himself), "Gator" (the nickname of Frost's codefendant, Whitaker), and "Cruz" (the nickname of another dealer). The government permitted Frost to help retrieve the evidence from his computer. A formal chain of custody for the computer records was not established. During the trial, Whitaker argued that the files implicating him through his alias were not properly authenticated. Whitaker argued that with a few keystrokes, Frost could have easily added Whitaker's alias, Gator, to the printouts in order to finger Whitaker and to appear more helpful to the government. Absent specific evidence that tampering with the records had occurred, the mere possibility of tampering does not affect the authenticity of a computer record. The courts rejected Frost's argument that the government failed to authenticate computer records when the government presented testimony of an FBI agent who was present when the records were retrieved.

Falsification

One form of falsification is called *spoofing*, which includes counterfeiting and man-in-the-middle attacks. Spoofing is a technique used to gain unauthorized access allowing an intruder to send to a computer with an IP address messages disguised as authentic messages originating from a trusted host. One spoof is to forge the "From" address so that the message appears to have been generated from somewhere other than its actual source.

Counterfeiting is a form of forgery where the identity of an organization is a spoofed identity that processes some type of document, such as one from the Social Security Administration. Counterfeiting sessions enable the bypass of authentication measures by tampering with requests and tricking the application into thinking that the attacker is already authenticated.

"Man-in-the-middle" attacks involve sniffing of packets from the network, changing them, and inserting them back into the network. *Sniffing* is computer software or hardware that intercepts, decodes and analyzes the contents of packets, and then logs the traffic passing through a network. The process begins with intercepting communication between two systems; for example, in the hypertext transfer protocol (HTTP) transaction the target is the TCP connection between client and server. HTTP is the underlying protocol used by the World Wide Web (WWW) defining how messages are formed and transmitted and what actions Web servers and browsers should take in response to the HTTP commands. TCP

is one of the main protocols in TCP/IP networks, enabling two hosts to establish a connection and exchange streams of data. Using different techniques, the attacker splits the original TCP connection into two new connections, one between the client and the attacker and the other between the attacker and the server (see Figure 5). Once the TCP connection is intercepted, the attacker acts as a proxy, able to read, insert, and modify the data in the intercepted communication.

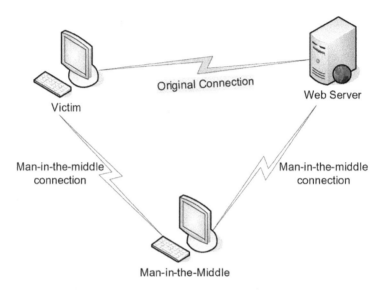

Figure 5. Man-in-the-Middle Attack Scenario

Superimposition

A cybercrime that involves silent penetration of a system to form opinions, manage perceptions, or foster deception using digitally enabled techniques is called a *superimposition* or *"morph"*. For example, when looking at an image of a downed commercial airliner, one might ask if the image is real or digitally mastered. The objective might not be to render the system inoperative or obliterate the system's information content, but to play mind games with the viewer. The objective is to be silent and invisible, leaving no external trace of the manipulation.

Confidentiality

Penetration

Common approaches to system penetration of targeted information systems, whether military, civil, or personal, are packet sniffers, password grabbers, password crackers, password guessing, and social engineering.[31] Hackers use several techniques to penetrate or compromise a system. A part of this process is for the hackers to cover their tracks. Methods typically used include giving the exploiting applications common names that are easy to conceal, looping by cracking into one system and using that system to breach a third system, and removing log entries. System penetration decreases the integrity of data and systems.

System penetration may come from within an organization or from outside. Common types include buffer overflow attacks, attacks against data, and the Port 80 problem. *Port 80* is used for Internet traffic and is often not protected by firewalls. Approximately 70% of all Web attacks exploit Port 80. In a buffer overflow attack, a hacker injects a remote system with so much data that the system is unable to handle the data and then bounces the hacker out into a command line such as the c:/prompt of a DOS-based system. From this point, the hacker can do much damage by issuing system-level commands that can erase huge chunks of data or retrieve passwords and other sensitive information. Attacks against data occur when hackers issue legitimate *structured query language* (SQL) commands in hopes that a database will act on them and retrieve the data they want, such as bank account information. SQL is a standardized query language for requesting information from a database.

Dial-up presents a huge exposure to attack. Dial-up is becoming less prevalent yet remains in use. While internal network protection through private networks is now less popular due to the high costs of installation, maintenance, and security, they remain common. An attacker who suspects that an organization has dial-up lines can use a device called a war dialer to locate the connection points.

With the growth of wireless LANs in the workplace, the wireless connection now represents the easiest backdoor to penetrate a network. Wireless connections have become the simplest vector to exploit, with businesses now beginning to understand the implications as regulatory compliance expands protection of sensitive information. As the complexity of wireless networks increases, attacks will become increasingly more sophisticated. The threats for wireless-specific products and protocols include IEEE (Institute of Electrical and Electronics Engineers) 802.11, Bluetooth, Enhanced Data Global System for Mobile Communications (GSM) Environment, High-Speed Downlink Packet Access, WiMax/802.16

Evolution-Data Optimized (EVDO), Voice over Wireless LAN (VoWLAN), and radio-frequency identification (RFID).

IEEE 802.11 is a group of specifications developed for wireless LAN technology. *Bluetooth* is a short-range radio technology that simplifies communications between Internet devices and the Internet. *Enhanced Data GSM Communications Environment* for digital cellular systems uses narrowband that allows multiple simultaneous calls on the same radio frequency. *High-Speed Downlink Packet Access* is a third-generation (3G) mobile telephony communications protocol that allows networks to have higher data transfer speeds and capacity. *WiMax/802.16* is an IEEE specification for fixed broadband wireless metropolitan access networks (MANs) using a point-to-multipoint architecture. *EVDO* is a fast wireless broadband access serving as a hotspot. *VoWLAN* is the use of a wireless broadband network for the purpose of vocal conversation. An automated identification method, *RFID,* depends on storing and remotely retrieving data using transponder devices or RFID tags.

Since the late 1990s, wired equivalent privacy (WEP) has been a wireless network security standard and the default method of securing Wi-Fi networks. Wi-Fi enables devices such as digital cameras, MP3 players, PDAs, PCs, and cell phones to connect directly with each other via a wireless connection. This secure wireless network technology has been replaced with *Wi-Fi Protected Access* (WPA, a wireless encryption standard), which is used by more than 40% of businesses and a significantly higher percentage of home users. WEP has many security problems and was blamed for the 2007 TJX Companies data breach that led to the compromise of 94 million credit card and debit card numbers. Attackers get close to the WEP-encrypted router, crack the WEP key used to encrypt network traffic, and log on to the network. Now the attacker has circumvented the firewall protection and attacks a laptop to set up a "man-in-the-middle" attack and snoop on the victim's online activity. This makes every individual on the wireless system the target of an attack.

Packet sniffers, also known as network monitors or network analyzers, are used to legitimately monitor and troubleshoot network traffic by network or system administrators. This information enables an administrator to identify erroneous packets, using the data to identify bottlenecks to help in maintaining efficient network data transmissions. The packet sniffer captures the packets that were intended for the machine in question. In the hands of an individual with malicious intent, with the same information and the same tool placed in the prominent mode, the system will capture all packets traversing the network regardless of destination. This enables the intruder to capture, view, and analyze all traffic, finding usernames and password information, typically in clear text.

Buffer overflows are application errors that occur when more data are sent than a buffer can handle. The attacker can then make the target system execute instructions at will. Most applications have some level of vulnerability to buffer overflows.

A relatively new kind of attack is the *timing attack*. Timing attacks explore Web browsers' cache contents, enabling the attacker to gather information on access to password-protected sites. Timing attacks also involve attempts to intercept cryptographic elements to discover keys and encryption algorithms.

Deviations in *quality of service* (QOS), a measure of a computer network or telephone service reliability, by service providers result in a product or service not delivered as expected. Internet service, communications, or power irregularities can cause availability of systems and information service issues. The interruption or loss of Internet services can create considerable loss in the availability of information, such as remote access to systems by telecommuters. Communications can be disrupted to and from many sources, including telecommunications, potable water, wastewater, trash, and cable services, for example. The threat of lost service can produce an inability to function correctly. Power irregularities include spikes (momentary increases), surges (prolonged increases), sags (momentary drops in voltage), brownouts (prolonged drops in voltage), faults (momentary losses of power), and blackouts (prolonged power losses).

Espionage

Espionage is a trespass that covers a broad category of activities focused on compromising confidentiality. Espionage, a form of spying, is the unauthorized access to sensitive information. Simple forms of espionage include shoulder surfing occurring when an individual is accessing confidential information with someone looking over his or her shoulder at the keystrokes used or information displayed.

In a September 2007 incident, Lan Lee and Yuefei Ge, of the San Francisco area, were charged by the U.S. attorney general's office with conspiracy to commit economic espionage and to steal trade secrets. Mr. Ge and Mr. Lee were alleged to have conspired to steal trade secrets from their employer, NetLogics Microsystems, and Taiwan Semiconductor Manufacturing Corporation, another company where the men were not employed. They were alleged to have created a company, SICO Microsystems, Inc., for the purpose of developing and marketing products derived from and using the stolen trade secrets. The trade secrets covered computer chip design and development. The defendants sought to obtain venture capital funding for their company from the government of China.

Misappropriation

Misappropriation of data for monetary gain can occur when systems have been compromised. Intruders steal sensitive information with the intent of profiting either through the sale of the stolen information to a competitor or through extortion. Misappropriation of resources for personal gain can occur by compromising a system and defacing the target's Web site, perhaps with the perpetrator proudly stating his or her own handle for good measure and for stature in the blackhat community. For example, an intruder informs a company that he or she has changed the logo and name of a firm's website to the perpetrator's name so that anyone that accesses the website sees the perpetrator's information rather than the firm's information.

Other Threats to Information Assets

Information extortion occurs when an attacker who steals data from a computer system and then demands compensation for its return, destruction, or exploit. Methods of extortion include requesting money, goods, or services by holding a hard disk ransom through encryption. For example, an intruder informs a company that he or she has obtained the credit card numbers of all its customers from the company's server and are holding this information ransom for $100,000.

Sabotage and vandalism involve an individual or group's deliberately sabotaging the operations of a system, or performing acts of vandalism that destroy an asset or damage the image of an organization. Threats from this form of cybercrime range from petty vandalism to organized sabotage, such as defacement of a company's Web site, and can result in declining consumer confidence and sales.

Compromise of intellectual property is a growing threat. *Intellectual property* is the ownership and control over the tangible or virtual representation of written or recorded media and ideas. Most organizations create and own intellectual property that should be safeguarded, such as trade secrets, copyrights, trademarks, and patents. A common breach involves software piracy and the failure to enforce copyrights. For example, Illinois State University used CopySense, a program to monitor illegal file sharing on its campus network. Files monitored included signatured files (music and video files with digital copyright information), files with metadata but no signatures (files with song titles that could indicate file sharing), and unknown files. Illinois State found that 2.9% were signatured files, and 28.4% were files with metadata, but no signatures, and 68.7% were unknown files. This means that more than 30% of the file sharing was most likely illegal.

Deliberate acts of theft involve the illegal taking of physical, intellectual, or electronic property belonging to another person. Electronic theft is typically more complex to manage and control than physical thefts. The reason is obvious when a machine is missing, less so when data stored electronically have been taken. In October 2007, the British and Dutch police in coordination with Interpol shut down what was one of the world's largest online sources of pirated music. The perpetrator, a twenty-four-year-old IT worker and Web site operator, was arrested in Middlesbrough in northeastern England. The Web site, OiNK, was an invitation-only Web site specializing in the distribution of albums that were leaked before their official release data by recording companies. OiNK's servers were in Amsterdam and were shut down by Dutch police. OiNK had approximately 180,000 members who paid donations to upload or download albums, sometimes weeks before their release. Within hours, these albums would be distributed across the Internet through public forums and blogs. To be invited, a requester had to prove he or she had music to share. In 2007, it was estimated that more than 60 major albums were leaked on OiNK, serving as a primary global source for illegal prerelease music. Prerelease piracy is extremely damaging to music sales, with early mixes and unfinished versions of an artist's recordings circulating on the Internet months before the final release. Hundreds of thousands of dollars were generated through the Web site.

Technological obsolescence occurs when a computer or the computing infrastructure becomes outdated, rendering the system untrustworthy or unreliable. To provide quality and to avoid technological obsolescence, an organization must invest sufficient funding for periodic conversion and migration of technology and the media used to store data.

Vulnerabilities

Vulnerabilities are weaknesses in a victim, be it a person, process, system, or technology that allow a threat to become effective. Vulnerabilities exist in all complex networked systems, wireless communications, and core wireless networking infrastructures such as access points (APs) and voice-over IP (VoIP) phones. Figure 6 shows four broad vulnerability zones for a computer system. The number of vulnerabilities will likely increase with the growing use of voice over wireless.

Vulnerability Zones

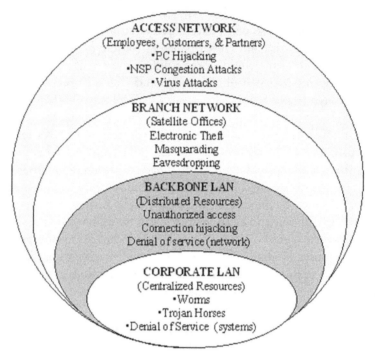

Figure 6. Computer Systems—Vulnerability Zones

A vulnerability model that reviews the countermeasures, vulnerability, threat, threat agent that leads to an exploit, attack and loss is shown in Table 6.

Table 6. Vulnerability Model

Term	Definition	Application	Examples
Countermeasures	A system designed to prevent an attack	Measures that counterattack or prevent an attack by destroying or altering the payload in such a manner that the intended effect is impeded or slowed	Antivirus software, biometrics, passwords

Term	Definition	Application	Examples
Vulnerability	An identified weakness of a controlled system that can be exploited by a threat	Concerns: ease of discovery and exploit, awareness, intrusion detection	Flaws or misconfigurations in the security of a system
Threat	The possibility an attacker will exploit a vulnerability to compromise an asset; an entity with both the capability and intention to exploit a vulnerability in an asset	Dependent on an attack, the presence of a vulnerability, and the possibility for exploitation	Deliberate software attacks, technical software or human failures or errors, deliberate acts of espionage/trespass, deliberate acts of sabotage/vandalism
Threat Agent	An individual or group that can manifest a threat; an attacker or malware that can exploit a vulnerability	Threat Agent = Capabilities + Intentions + Past Activities	Computer viruses, worms, employees, organized crime and criminals; human intentional and unintentional actions; natural events (fires, earthquakes, floods)
Exploit	A technique to compromise a system; a process or tool that will attack a vulnerability in an asset	Takes advantage of a vulnerability to cause unintended or unanticipated behaviors	Malware, viruses, Trojans, root-kits, <bob check: "rootkit" earlier?>worms
Attack	A deliberate act that exploits a vulnerability	Accomplished by a threat agent	Backdoors, brute force, DDoS, man-in-the-middle, virus, Trojan, social engineering, password crack
Loss	A successful intrusion or breach of a computer system	Loss expectancy in terms such as monetary loss, productivity loss, and reputation	Financial, including penalties and fines, litigation, damage to reputation, loss of customers

A *risk* is a concept symbolizing a potential negative impact to an asset (the vulnerability) that may arise from a current or future event (the threat). In short, a risk is the exposure to a threat resulting from a vulnerability. The *loss expectancy* from a risk includes the improper use of technology, the inability to control technology, and the inability to react in a timely manner, all of which could lead to the concentration of data and incorrect data entry. The loss expectancy is the expected monetary loss that can be expected due to a risk over time.

THREAT x VULNERABILITY = RISK

Vulnerabilities are inherent in all types of technologies. To exploit a vulnerability, the attacker must locate the target, plan and execute the attack, and then escape. Location and access are the keys to exploiting a vulnerability. This process can be reduced to these steps:

1. Identify target and gather information.
    Example: identify a host and IP ranges domain named server (DNS) used, and then identify OS.

2. Identify and analyze vulnerability.
    Example: use hacking tools to identify local and remote vulnerabilities.

3. Acquire appropriate level of access to the target.
    Example: to gain system level access on a server, insert a Trojan for later entry even if passwords are changed.

4. Carry out attack.
    Example: do whatever you want to do as a hacker, such as defacement, deletion, or spying.

5. Erase evidence and avoid retaliation.
    Example: Use a bot controlled computer to delete logs.

Exploits

Exploits are hacker attacks on known vulnerabilities. Staying abreast of what vulnerabilities exist and discovering what new or previously undiscovered ones apply in both legacy and upgraded systems is critical to the ongoing security of a business. Exploits are pieces of software, data, or sequences of command that take advantage of vulnerabilities, bugs, or glitches to gain control of a system or allow privileges to applications or users protecting resources or privileges. Classification of exploits are based on (a) how the exploit contacts the vulnerable software remote or local exploit, (b) the type of vulnerability an exploit attacks, or (c) by the action against a vulnerable system. Typically, known exploits target known vulnerabilities. For example, some Web sites on the Internet provide both novice and expert computer hackers with exploits needed to conduct attacks. Anyone can download the hacker tools and instructions for his or her use. The exploits downloaded from these Web sites may be used to deface Web pages, create or delete files and e-mails, or modify security features on a computer system once the hacker is logged in as a trusted system user.

Common exploits are defects in Internet browsers that allow the installation of adware, spyware, or other malicious programs on computers, which are then used to visit malicious or compromised Web sites. Exploits such as spam and worms can also be installed by clicking links in e-mail messages that lead to malicious or compromised Web sites. These are examples of exploits where the installation may occur without operator intervention or notification once the Web site is visited.

Known exploits are usually published through both ethical and unethical sources. A patch is used to fix the vulnerability, rendering the exploit obsolete for newer versions of an application. Zero day exploits are kept private by the malicious hacker(s), then released before or on the same day the vulnerability is published or the vendor patch is available to the public. The term *zero day* refers to the number of days between any public advisory of the vulnerability and the release of the exploit, which is zero. Exploits based on the vulnerability of an exploit attack include buffer overflows, race condition, code injection, cross-site scripting, and cross-site request forgery.

An exploit may be used to expand influence by providing superuser-level access to a computing system immediately or by elevating privileges repeatedly at a low-level access until the root has been reached by taking advantage of buffer-over-run holes or by sending large amounts of data to determine network intrusion detection systems (NIDS) thresholds. The increase in network utilization and the number of critical application layers exploits means that NIDS designers must create new methods for rapid attack analysis techniques when monitoring a fully saturated network and maintaining a false positive to false negative ratio. With these types of exploits, hackers can clean up to cover their tracks and hide any evidence of intrusion within log files.

Exploits may also be used for profit, for example, by stealing information by accessing sensitive files typically stored in the default "My Documents" folder on Windows client machines. Hackers with access to these systems can steal sensitive data such as credit card numbers and passwords for malicious intent. A hacker may also use an accessed modem to dial out unnoticed to 900 numbers that charge by the minute in a remote country, running up charges on telephone accounts. Exploits are also used on client browsers to point the default Web site to a malicious site.

CHAPTER 4

CYBERCRIME AND INFORMATION TECHNOLOGY

Behind the prevention and prosecution of cybercrime looms the larger challenge of creating a global culture of cybersecurity, addressing the needs of all societies, including developing countries, with their emerging and still vulnerable information technology structures.

Cybercrime incidents are also known as computer security breaches. A computer security breach is by law ambiguous. In the United States, the law states that a computer security breach is the unauthorized acquisition of computerized data that compromises the security, confidentiality, or integrity of personal information maintained by an individual or business entity. A computer security breach occurs, for example, when an outside hacker gains unauthorized access to a system or when an employee obtains personal information from an employer's computer system that is not required to perform his or her duties.

The types of security problems related to cybercrime that create financial losses are many. Four major sources are inadvertent errors, malicious employees, malicious outsiders, and industrial espionage. Inadvertent errors come have many sources, from a user innocently downloading a screen saver that contains malicious code to a well-meaning developer introducing errors that cause downtime or open a security hole in the production environment that enables subsequent attacks by related third parties. Most businesses are "boundary free," with networked computing, proliferation of the Internet, and automated software attracting, motivating, and enabling hackers, criminals (malicious outsiders), and malicious insiders to attack and misuse business applications for malice and profit. Traditional security measures aimed at protecting a network are inadequate in protecting the software or the business. Industrial espionage ranges from the traditional methods of covert data gathering through the execution of corporate technology agreements to obtain valuable information, exploiting Internet discussion groups and requesting information through e-mail, Customs officials holding laptops for an extended time, to dumpster diving, or intercepting nonencrypted Internet messages.

The number and types of tools used to bring injury to computers and networks are many and include passwords, software flaws, hardware, spyware, wireless LANs, e-mail, and broadband connections. The careless use and storage of passwords by authorized users, delivery of malicious code, exploitation of security flaws, patches in software, exploitation of vulnerabilities in hardware, and the use of snooping with cookies in the form of adware or spyware may easily lead to a cybercrime incident. The IEEE standard for wireless security, 802.1x, has its share of flaws in that one can access an open wireless network from a public place, and with the placement of snooping data packets, the individual can obtain access to computers, networks, and the data stored on the open wireless network. Computer hardware comes with default passwords. Failure to change these passwords during the installation process can leave a system vulnerable to attack.

Spyware is computer software secretly installed on a computer to intercept or seize partial control over the user's interaction with the computer, without the user's informed consent. Spyware typically does not self-replicate; rather, it exploits infected computers for commercial gain, such as by displaying paid advertisements. Spyware gains access to a system through deception or exploitation of software vulnerabilities. Spyware can lead to degradation of system performance and unwanted behavior. Examples of spyware are Moviepass.tx and Popcorn.net, movie download services that have generated thousands of complaints to the FTC, BBB, and state attorneys general.

Wireless LANs (WLANs) are wireless local area networks that link two or more computers without using wires. WLANs are convenient, mobile, easy to install and deploy, expandable, and continue to decrease in costs. WLANs cover relatively short ranges that are adequate for home users but insufficient for large buildings. Reliability suffers from periods of weak signals due to interference and complex propagation effects that are beyond the control of network administrations.

Electronic mail (e-mail) and use of anonymous e-mail programs, such as Anonymizer, make it difficult or unlikely to be able to trace the source of an e-mail that is used to launch a DDoS attack or exploit the SMTP port on open servers on the Internet. Sending an e-mail from a false e-mail address, known as fraudulent or spoof e-mail, can launch such attacks. Spoofing can result in thousands of replies to the return address, potentially shutting down the server due to the increased traffic generated. *Phishing* is malicious code or requests for personal sensitive information from unsuspecting end users via e-mail. Increases in the use of broadband connections and the slow adoption of personal firewalls on computers have rendered these computers vulnerable to a variety of attacks that are often random and accessed by hackers to launch other types of attacks or to gain access to the user's network of computers.

Broadband Internet connections deliver high-speed Internet access compared to dial-up access over a modem. Dial-up modems are limited to 56 kilobits per second (kbit/s) and require the full use of a telephone line. Conversely, broadband technologies are at least twice the speed of dial-up and generally do not disrupt telephone use.

Multiple perspectives exist on when and under what circumstances a business should report a computer security breach. In California, for example, Senate Bill (SB) 1386 states that a business is required to give, within 48 hours, notice of a discovery of a security breach to a law enforcement agency. As of 2007, Texas did not have a mandate in existence; rather, businesses were merely encouraged to notify law enforcement. Many businesses report a computer security breach to law enforcement only when mandated by law or when the severity of a computer security breach is significant enough to bring potential harm to the organization's reputation or to a large segment of its customers. The U.K. Fraud Act of 2006 states that victims of bank fraud must notify the financial institution directly rather than the police. The financial institution is the institution that decides to report the details to the police, which gives financial institutions too much discretion over what types of fraud are reported and investigated by the police. In India, it has been recommended before a parliamentary standing committee that the liability of ISPs for any third-party content be raised in a manner that would make it difficult to run the service and stay out of jail. The intention is make ISPs potentially responsible for content on blogs, mail services, and search engines that could be legitimately confiscated by the police but for which ISPs have limited or no responsibility.

Significant gaps exist in the literature due to the level of reporting of cybercrime incidents by organizations and the level of record keeping maintained by law enforcement agencies. The true severity of cybercrime is underestimated, showing the need for education, innovation, policies, and support to encourage organizations to report incidents and help fight cybercrime.

Computer Infrastructure and Security Technology

A primary tool of the workplace for conducting business and exchanging information is the computer infrastructure and security technology of information technology (IT). Likewise, consumers and business leaders want protection of their sensitive and personal information stored and used electronically. The computer infrastructure and security posture of an organization can become an attractive target for cybercriminals. These factors and the ease of access to sensitive and personal data drive the policies, behaviors, and decisions made by business and government leaders.

From one perspective, IT computer infrastructure and security technology provide a convenient forum for "anytime, anywhere" access to required information by those who need it quickly. The use of IT leads to faster responses to queries, such as extension of credit within minutes of completing an application online.

In contrast, anywhere, anytime access that is used to provide quick extension of credit due to the ease of online access to personal financial data requires vigilant authentication of the identification of the individual providing the information. This ensures that credit is granted only to the party intended by the business rather than to a criminal. Anywhere, anytime access to this data allows a criminal to assume another individual's identity to acquire goods online. The criminal needs only a valid name and Social Security number to establish credit under an assumed alias online. To restrict unauthorized access to a system authentication of a user is needed.

Authentication: One Factor, Two Factors, or Multifactors

Authentication is about restricting unauthorized access to a system by requiring authorized users to prove their identity. The ideal authentication tools satisfy all three factors: (a) something you know (password or PIN), (b) something you have (magnetic strip, driver's license, medical card), (c) and something unique to you (your palm print, fingerprint, or signature). Using a combination of these measures increases the security of the system.

Table 7. Authentication Methods

Number of Methods	Authentication	Strength	Example
1	One-factor	Weak	Password or PIN
2 or more	Two-factors or Multifactors	Strong	One factor and one or more of the following: token, biometric, mobile telephone, smart card, USB token, virtual token, one-time password token

One-Factor Authentication

One-factor authentication seeks to satisfy one of the three factors for authenticating a user. One-factor authentication is the most common security system and can be compromised by using several techniques including dictionary attacks, brute force attacks, password grabbers, default passwords, observation, obvious passwords, indiscretion, or social engineering. One-factor authentication is considered a weak authentication security system.

Passwords are a form of secret authentication data used to control access to a resource. The password remains secret from those not allowed access and access is granted to those who know the correct password. A *personal identification number* (PIN) is a passcode, a numeric password commonly used for ATM access.

Password cracking is an attempt to try as many times as possible to learn a valid password. A *dictionary attack* uses every word in the dictionary to guess the password, considered an efficient method of password discovery. Dictionary attacks may also check for multiple words used together (e.g., mymotherisnice), words spelled backward (e.g., rehtom), and words with numbers appended (added at the end, such as "mother1") or prepended to a word (added at the beginning such as "1mother"). The most common password in use today is "password1." A *brute force attack* tries every combination of every letter in the alphabet and other characters, a time-consuming approach.

Password grabbers intercept passwords once they have been typed. This is accomplished by capturing the password as it travels along networks. A second approach is to use a program that records every key pressed on a PC, a *keylogger*. A third approach is to use a program that emulates a login prompt asking the user to enter his login ID and password information. The login ID and password are then sent on to another party for use.

Default passwords are commonly built into many systems. New accounts are often given a default password (e.g., new employee IDs) using the name as the password. If not changed immediately, these can easily be exploited. *Observations* come from watching an individual type his or her password and login ID on a system. Obvious passwords are the account holder's name, nickname, names of friends, spouses, or animals, or other words that can be easily guessed. Indiscretion comes from writing down passwords and placing the password in an unlocked drawer, on top of a desk where it may be found easily, or by telling someone your password.

Social engineering is used to trick unsuspecting employees into revealing system names and addresses, login IDs, and password information using false pretenses, typically over the telephone. For example, the perpetrator will call pretending to be a system administrator having problems at his or her end and request the victim's password to repair the problem. A system administrator does not have a need for a user's password. Even when an organization is strong from a technology perspective, with the best technology in place, including firewalls, intrusion-detection systems, biometric devices, and so on, people remain the weakest link.

Two-Factor or Multifactor Authentication

Two-factor authentication (T-FA) (or multifactor authentication) is an authentication system using two or more different methods to validate a user. Using at least two factors rather than just one, such as a password, delivers a higher level of authentication insurance, referred to as strong authentication. T-FA uses "something you know" (e.g., a password) as one of at least two factors, and uses either "something you have" (a physical device, e.g., a credit card) or "something you are" (a biometric) as another factor. Common examples of T-FA are credit cards and debit cards. The card is something you have and the PIN is something you know. A poorly implemented T-FA process may be less secure than a properly deployed one-factor authentication process.

Strong authentication and multifactor authentication are fundamentally different processes. Soliciting multiple answers to challenge questions may be considered strong authentication, yet the process must also retrieve "something you have" or "something you are" for it to be considered multifactor. In 2006, the Federal Financial Institutions Examination Council (FFIEC) issued supplemental guidance on authentication. The FFIEC states that "… true multifactor authentication requires the use of solutions from two or more of the three categories of factors. Using multiple solutions from the same category … would not constitute multifactor authentication." As the use of T-FA expands, businesses and consumers should experience a reduction in online identity theft and other cybercrimes, because a password alone would not be enough to access a system.

Despite its strength, T-FA is vulnerable to Trojans and man-in-the-middle attacks. Another issue regarding deployment of T-FA is that some users experience difficulty keeping track of another object. A third issue is that many T-FA solutions are proprietary and protected by patents, resulting in higher costs. Passwords and PINs commonly used in one-factor authentication solutions do not have an annual fee per person, common among many of the T-FA solutions. A fourth concern is that T-FA is not standardized, causing interoperability issues. Additional costs include implementation, maintenance, and replacement of damaged or lost devices such as tokens.

Company Investments in Security Technology

For many organizations, the way logical security investments are measured compared to the way investments are made for the remainder of the organization differs. The difference between how investments are made and measured makes it difficult for organizations to determine how much to invest on logical security. The level of investment is typically driven by the level of risk aversion a firm is willing to accept.

The scope of economic damages resulting from cybercrime should not be limited to actual computer outage and employees being unable to perform their tasks. The economic damages caused by cybercrime ought to be assessed on broad terms as even the impact of a single cybercrime incident may have perpetual ramifications. The economic harm from a single cybercrime incident can be staggering. Understanding the economic damage of a single cybercrime incident is important when assessing the risk of a cybercrime incident on an organization. For example, in 2002 Hurricane Andrew caused approximately $25 billion dollars worth of damage while the Love Bug virus cost computer users globally $6.7 billion in damages in the first five days[32] and as much as $15 billion during the reporting period.[33] Remarkably, a single university student in the Philippines caused the Love Bug using inexpensive computer equipment.

Some organizations evaluate return on investment (ROI) or return on security investment (ROSI) using data gathered during a cost-benefit analysis. These organizations weigh the price of security options to their potential benefit, then select the security alternative that yields the highest returns. An organization is more likely to invest in logical security if the organization has either (1) experienced cybercrime resulting in more attention from senior management, or (2) has leaders who are sensitive to the need for security and are willing to spend more on prevention. Some organizations place a low priority on cybercrime prevention because they have yet to experience any sizeable losses due to cybercrime.

Return on Investment

ROI is a popular financial tool for measuring the economic return of an investment or project. ROI calculates the gain from investment minus the cost of an investment, collectively divided by the cost of the investment. Many businesses will pursue an investment that has a positive ROI within a given period of time. For example, if an investment has a positive ROI during its first year, the business will approve this project over a project that has a negative ROI in its first year. The formula for ROI is

ROI = (Gain from Investment - Cost of Investment) ÷ Cost of Investment

For example:

Project A:
0.61 = ($380,190 - $236,874) ÷ $236,874
➔ This Project has a positive ROI

Project B:
-0.48 = ($123,190 - $236,874) ÷ $236,874
➔ This Project has a negative ROI

The business will approve Project A that has a positive ROI over Project B which has a negative ROI.

Net benefits or *gain* from an investment, are the profit, earnings, or future income for the first year or is the difference between the benefits of the investment and the associated costs used to generate the benefits, with or without taxes and depreciation. The value of ROI is lower if taxes and depreciation are included, yet arguably a more accurate figure. The formula for net benefits is

Net Benefits = Gain on Investment - Cost of Investment

Using the example above, the net benefit or loss from Project A and B are as follows:

Project A:
$143,316 = $380,190 - $236,874
➔ This Project has a net benefit of $143,316.

Project B:
($113,684) = $123,190 - $236,874
➔ This Project has a net loss of ($113,684).

Costs include all costs incurred to obtain the net benefits of the investment or project. This may be called invested capital, invested assets, or total project costs for the first year or calculated as a weighted average of invested capital during the lifetime of the investment.

Return on Security Investment

ROSI considers the return on a security investment based on an expected loss in a year from an intrusion or security breach. The formula for ROSI is

$$\textbf{ROSI} = \text{ROSI} = [(E \times M) - C] \div C$$

Where

E is the cost per year to recover from any number of security breaches.

M is the percentage of risks mitigated by stopping any number of security breaches through the introduction of a security tool.

C is the cost of the security tool.

Table 8. ROSI—Hypothetical Situation

Hypothetical Situation:
Company XYZ recently experienced a virus that shut down operations for one hour. The estimated cost in damages and lost productivity resulting from the virus infection was $25,000. Company XYZ has experienced four virus infections this year and anticipates at least four more virus outbreaks next year. Company XYZ plans to purchase anti-virus software at a cost of $25,000 which includes implementation and professional services. Should Company XYZ invest in the antivirus software?
Calculate the ROSI:
ROSI = [(E x M) - C] ÷ C
(E) Risk Exposure: $25,000 x 4/annually = $100,000
(M) Risk Mitigated: 75%
(C) Solution Cost: $25,000
200% = [($100,000 x 75%) - $25,000] ÷ $25,000
ROSI = 200%

Yes, Company XYZ should purchase the antivirus software since the ROSI is positive.

ROSI measures how survivability of attacks increases as security spending is increased. ROSI is a curve reflecting the trade-off between what you spend and how safe you are, a form of regression analysis as defined by economists. Using the hypothetical situation above, at first glance the antivirus software is worth the investment when assuming the cost of a cybercrime incident is estimated at $25,000. The ROSI worsens if the damages from the cybercrime event is less, such as $5,000. The ROSI in this case would be a negative 40% therefore the investment in antivirus software would appear to not be worth the investment. Conversely, if the cost of a cybercrime incident is estimated at $35,000 per incident, the ROSI improves to 320% signaling that the investment in the antivirus software is a wise choice.

Some organizations delay investment in new technology to reduce the need for investment in security technology. For example, the Federal Aviation Association (FAA) has ninety major computer systems and nine different communications networks using aged equipment and proprietary software. This approach makes the FAA communications networks difficult targets to hack externally. This approach has led to very few reports of attacks affecting air traffic, yet a single incident can cause potentially significant harm. For example, one incident of cybercrime involved a young hacker who successfully interrupted local telephone service, cut off a regional airport's control tower, and eliminated its ability to turn on runway lights in the New England region. This interruption lasted six hours, without an accident. A similar breach at a national airport could have led to potential loss of life and millions of dollars in damage. In summary, the level of risk tolerance held by business leaders determines how much an organization will invest in security technology.

Computer Downtime

Computer downtime refers to a period or a percentage of a time span that a computer system is not available or functioning, usually due to a system failure or planned maintenance. The costs for computer downtime are illustrated in Table 9 below and can be calculated as follows:

Step 1: Total Hours of Downtime X Hourly Wage of Each
         Affected Worker = Lost Wages

Step 2: Number of Hours to Service the Device X Cost per Hour for
         Repair = Cost of Service

Step 3: Lost Wages + Cost of Service = Total Cost of Downtime

Table 9. Computer Downtime Cost Calculation

Computer Downtime Cost Calculation (per Personal Computer [Client])			
	Type of Service		
	On-site	Drop-off	Remote
Total Downtime	8 Hours	20 Hours	2 Hours
Lost Wages ($35/hr.)	$280	$700	$70
Cost of Service (2 hrs.)	$200	$120	$160
Total Cost of Downtime	$480	$820	$230

The formula used to calculate the cost of downtime for PCs can also be applied to servers. The cost of service and wages may be higher. The hourly rates are industry averages for an IT worker and the cost of service. Wages and costs may vary depending on the specific situation.

Some organizations prefer to track computer uptime, the opposite of computer downtime. Computer uptime is the time a system is working without failure. The measure typically sought for important systems within an organization is 99.0% or higher; for mission-critical systems, this percentage may average as much as 99.9999% uptime for a data center supporting critical national infrastructures such as telecommunications that support the Internet, the electrical power grid, or the NASA space shuttle mission. These systems are classified as managed through ultra-high availability. Unmanaged systems, having system availability of 90%, are typically found in use by consumers and small businesses.

Computer uptime is referred to as RAS (reliability, availability, serviceability) and ranges from ultrahigh availability to unmanaged systems. Ultrahigh availability systems range from self-healing with components designed for continuous processing without interruption to unmanaged systems that may remain unavailable for weeks at a time and where standard recovery processes are applied.

The economic and noneconomic impact of computer downtime is increasing as computers have become more powerful, complex, and managed by a growing number of IT workers, raising its relative importance to an organization. An hour of computer downtime for a stock brokerage firm can cost it $6 million or more. Computer downtime goes beyond the time span a system is offline or not functioning; it also encompasses the consequences to businesses, in terms of both economic and noneconomic damages. Computer downtime is also a place to begin determining the estimated extent of unplanned outages to computing systems.

Noneconomic damages include loss of privacy, loss of access to confidential data and systems, the unavailability or downgrade in system performance, and even the revelation of previously unknown information. These are harms that are more difficult to value monetarily and may not require the victim to make any financial expenditures. Businesses, consumers, and government have difficulty calculating the cost of computer intrusions or computer viruses. Standardized guidelines or methodologies are not available on how to measure these intangibles.

Risk Management and Compliance

For an organization to mitigate cybercrime, it must implement some level of risk management. The first step is to identify the probability and frequency of risks associated with potential vulnerabilities and threats. These risks are used to define the scope of the enterprise risk management (ERM) program, which incorporates issues of detection, prevention, and how to manage an attack. If an attack is identified, then the breach is quickly classified as to type. Next, a review of information assets that are at stake are assessed for vulnerability and the ERM program is activated, including quarantine and elimination of the breach. ERM is always on, in that ERM is in place before, during, and after an incident. ERM also addresses the prevention of an attack through technology, processes, and resource plans as depicted in Figure 7.

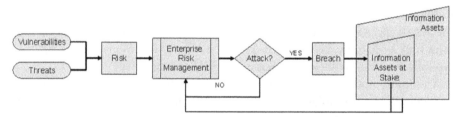

Figure 7. High-level Risk Management Workflow

Regulatory compliance has influenced security practices of businesses, and to a lesser degree, that of consumers (see Appendix B. Common Risk Management Methodologies). The regulatory landscape has pressured businesses to adopt a more structured approach to information security. Business technology professionals spend nearly one day a week addressing industry and government-related issues according to a study conducted by *Information Week* in 2005.[34] Compliance has yielded positive changes, including documenting of internal controls, establishing records-retention schedules, and reengineering of current applications to support applicable compliance efforts. Regulatory compliance and risk management programs have made organizations more cautious based on their established information security program or lack of such a program.

Two major dimensions of risk are probability and impact. Risk involves uncertainty (probability), and risk affects objectives (the impact). Risks can be neutral with an undefined impact or can include both threats and opportunities. In terms of cybercrime, individuals are more likely to be early adopters, which increase their risks. Early adopters typically purchase new technology as soon as it becomes available and before any updates or patches have been released to address bugs in the product. It is the joy of being first with new technology that generally motivates their buying habits. Conversely, organizations lag in adopting newer technologies and are typically slower to respond. Organizations typically wait until a product has been thoroughly tested elsewhere in the market and within their own testing environment. This process allows an organization to identify bugs that could lead to a vulnerability before the product has been installed. Another factor is that there are generally more processes and computers where a product will be deployed requiring more effort in deploying the product.

Organizations that address risk as an integrated process of threats and opportunities typically have stronger risk management programs and tend to support change. On the other hand, organizations with a threat-only focus have a risk process focused exclusively on threats and are less supporting of change. To view risk as both an opportunity and a threat, organizations should continuously change their thinking and their language, modify processes, and adapt standards as needed.

To change the way an organization thinks, the organization should review what could go wrong, how bad it could become, and how the organization can do better. To change its language, the organization can avoid, transfer, reduce, or mitigate risks as well as exploit, share, maximize, or enhance risks. The new language is that risk is the effect of uncertainty on objectives to be managed appropriately, rather than "risk is a potential problem to be minimized or avoided." Many processes, tools, and techniques are available to address identification, assessment, and response planning to risks. In addition, many standards are available to choose from to address the risks associated with cybercrime.

Cryptography

Cryptography is the study of or the protection of information through hiding or transforming data so that it is in an unintelligible format such as encrypting passwords within an application. *Encryption* is the process of converting an original message into a form that is unreadable by unauthorized individuals. Cryptography is an important component of secure information and communications systems, and a variety of applications have been developed that incorporate cryptographic methods to provide data security. Cryptography is an effective tool for ensuring both the confidentiality and the integrity of data, and each of these uses offers certain benefits. However, the widespread use of cryptography raises a number of important issues. Governments have wide-ranging responsibilities, several of which are specifically implicated in the use of cryptography, including protecting the privacy rights of their citizens; facilitating information and communications systems security; encouraging economic well-being by, in part, promoting electronic commerce; maintaining public safety; raising revenues to finance their activities; and enabling the enforcement of laws and the protection of national security. Although legitimate governmental, commercial, and individual needs and uses for cryptography are available, it may also be used by individuals or entities for illegal activities, which can affect public safety, national security, and the enforcement of laws, business interests, consumer interests, and privacy. Governments, together with industry and the public, are challenged to develop balanced policies to address these issues.

Cryptography and encryption are sophisticated approaches to security. Many security-related tools use embedded encryption technologies. The science of encryption, known as *cryptology*, encompasses cryptography and cryptanalysis. *Cryptography*, from a data security perspective, includes the need for keeping sensitive information confidential, detection of changes to data that affect data integrity, authentication of users, and nonrepudiation, preventing the denial of an authorized action. *Cryptanalysis* involves the study of mathematical methods used to defeat cryptographic techniques.

Many studies have shown that the full potential of electronic commerce will not be realized until public key infrastructures emerge that generate sufficient trust for businesses and individuals to commit their information and transactions to the emerging public networks. Few jurisdictions have adopted specific legislation for certificate infrastructures at present; however, a number of countries are looking at this issue, considering regulations and licensing procedures for certificate authorities.

CHAPTER 5

COUNTERMEASURES FOR CYBERSPACE

Like parking in a dangerous part of town, you find a well-lit street, lock your car, and then carry on your business. The same precaution should apply to a computer system. A 50% reduction in your risk is significant by any statistical measure. Pay some now or pay much more later!

It is important to understand what needs to be protected and then develop a plan to protect sensitive data using available technology, processes, policies, and laws. Cyberspace requires layers of support from both the people and technology perspectives. There are four layers of protection to consider from the technology perspective: data, the computing system, networks, and the Internet. People make the difference at all levels of protection. People using computing systems must be aware of their environment. Security planning, laws, and education can increase awareness. Cyberspace is limited only by access controls provided through the four layers of technology protection, which are used to connect a computing device as illustrated in Figure 8.

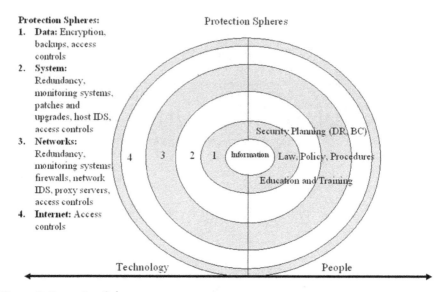

Protection Spheres:
1. **Data:** Encryption, backups, access controls
2. **System:** Redundancy, monitoring systems, patches and upgrades, host IDS, access controls
3. **Networks:** Redundancy, monitoring systems, firewalls, network IDS, proxy servers, access controls
4. **Internet:** Access controls

Figure 8. Protection Spheres.

Note. Adapted from Department of Information Technology, Kennesaw State University, 2006.

Prevent: Make Exploits Difficult

The focus on prevention is to make exploits difficult, because total elimination of a cyberthreat is not possible. A summary of defense approaches is shown in Table 10.

Table 10. Defensive Approaches in Using Technology

	Defensive Approaches Using Technology	
Make Exploits Difficult	Firewalls and Proxies	Network Segmentation
	Screening Routers	Encryption
	Intrusion Prevention	Certification
	Configuration Control	Security Leader
	Information Security Program	Business Continuity

Firewalls and Proxies

A *firewall* is a protective device that sits on the network using a set of rules to govern inbound and outbound traffic in and out of the network. The rules restrict access between the protected network and the Internet or other networks, such as an intranet or extranet. Firewalls typically function on at least one of three OSI layers—network/IP, TCP, and the application layer. It is recommended that firewalls be established to enhance security at each of these layers rather than just a single layer to provide a strong defense against an attack.

Network/IP layer firewalls control packet flows, blocking whatever is not explicitly allowed. Network/IP layer firewalls are designed for speed—packet contents are not analyzed, allowing the packets to be processed faster. The network/IP layer firewall is vulnerable to buffer overruns and IP spoofing attacks.

TCP layer firewalls operate at the session level, relaying TCP connections without extra processing. TCP layer firewalls require modified clients to communicate with the gateway. Internal and external computers do not have direct connections between each other.

The most secure type of firewall is the *application layer firewall,* which is configured to be the only host address visible to the external network. All connections to the internal network must clear this firewall. Application layer firewalls use proxies for services such as HTTP that prevent direct access to services on the internal network.

Proxy services provide Internet access to one or a few hosts for the computers that do not have the access. Requests are evaluated by the proxy service to determine which may pass and those to be discarded. Passed requests are relayed from the client to the real server, and the real server will relay an answer back to the client, protecting the real server on the Internet, as shown in Figure 9.

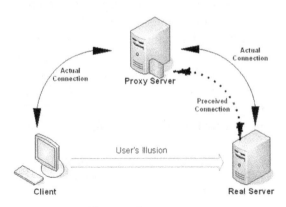

Figure 9. Proxy server.

Screening Routers

Screening routers work within the screened host architecture where packet filtering serves as the primary security. Packet filtering prevents one from making a direct connection by going around proxy servers. A screening router is placed between the private network and the Internet, blocking all traffic between the two networks except that authorized within the system (see Figure 10).

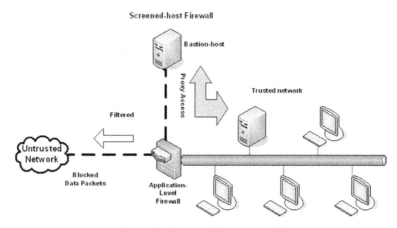

Figure 10. Screened-host Firewall

Intrusion Prevention

Businesses must ensure that the correct emphasis is placed on security, including intrusion prevention. Intrusion prevention systems allow the administrator to detect and block attacks from a reactive perspective. This means that intrusion prevention will stop attacks from being successful but does not prevent attacks. Many of the intrusion prevention solutions offered give false positives that lead to blocking legitimate traffic. To minimize the impact, fine-tuning of the environment is required. Having both firewalls for access control and an intrusion detection system (IDS) for monitoring network traffic is better than having only one of the two. The likelihood of a successful attack remains high if other security measures are not implemented as a part of a comprehensive information security program.

Intrusion prevention systems are effective protection for network and application-layer attacks. These systems can block known and unknown attacks, will not block legitimate traffic when under attack, and can provide relevant data for forensic analysis and alert reporting.

Configuration Control

Systems today should be designed, operated, and managed to respond to rapid technical and operational developments, unlike in the past when configuration control focused on keeping a network static, even at the risk of technical and operational obsolescence. According to the Joint Council on Information Age Crime, *configuration controls* are processes for modifying software, hardware, firmware, and documentation to ensure protection of an information system against improper changes before, during, and after a system has been implemented.[35]

Information Security Program and Risk Management

Likely sources of cybercrime are employees, former employees, and hackers. Building a comprehensive information security program needed to minimize the risk of becoming a cybercrime victim requires people, processes, and technology. People from all levels of the organization are active participants in the preventative model. The effort is led by the individual assigned as the chief security officer (CSO), chief privacy officer (CPO), or chief information security officer (CISO). Processes begin with an overall security strategy that is used as a baseline for employees, customer, partners, and a centralized security information management (SIM) system. SIM software automates the collection of event log data from security devices that are normalized and presented through a common management console for users to review. The technology needed for a comprehensive information security program includes firewalls, encryption, an IDS, antivirus and other detection software, data backup, user security and identification management, an intrusion prevention system (IPS) and filters, and Internet security.

Information security serves several purposes for an organization, including:

1. protecting an organization's ability to function,

2. enabling the safe operation of applications functioning on the organization's IT systems,

3. protecting the data the organization gathers and uses, and

4. safeguarding technology assets used by the organization.

Figure 11. Elements of Information Security

Elements of an information security management program begin with an understanding of the information assets within an organization. Next is to develop a plan that provides prevention, detection, and a response plan in the event of an incident. The process is continuous beginning and ending with awareness. Awareness drives the need for assessment of the environment, then designing countermeasures. The countermeasures are implemented and monitoring begins. Monitoring can lead to early detection of an incident. Once an incident has occurred the investigative process begins. The exploited and vulnerable environments are contained through limitations recommended from the investigation or the exploit itself. Once an incident has been identified, recovery efforts begin. Using all of the information gained and interviewing parties involved in any corrective measures, a review and documentation of lessons learned is needed. Documentation of the lessons learned leads to enhancements to the awareness program. This flow is depicted in Figure 11.

Information Security Management Structure

Key components of an information security management program are the security vision and strategy, senior management commitment, processes, incorporation of a training and awareness program, and a security management structure. The security vision and strategy should have a documented mission statement with guiding principles and the philosophy stated. The strategy should address information protection and define a security committee as an authoritative decision and communication vehicle. The strategy should consider the risk drivers by providing a view of the technology strategy and usage, business initiatives and processes, and a review of potential threats defined from a vulnerability and risk assessment within the organization.

The commitment from senior management is the stated and modeled commitment in principle and in practice. The information security program should be supported through policy and standards, directives, and resource allocation. The senior management commitment should also include a determination of risk tolerance as defined by requirements, policy, and standards. These should be in alignment with the classification and control of information.

The architecture and solutions used within an organization's infrastructure should incorporate security architecture and technical security standards that are used to develop, deploy, and integrate enforcement, monitoring, recovery, and response processes. These processes must be maintained and staff trained so they are functional. Each of these processes should address the resources necessary. The framework includes a training and awareness program for all individuals and vendors. Collectively the risk drivers, requirements, standards and alignment, architecture and solutions, people, processes, and methodology are the major components of the information security management structure.

The many regulations around the world such as Basel II, FFIEC guidelines, and SOX have shifted the focus of information technology from an IT concern to a corporate concern covering information security and data integrity for all levels of an organization (see Appendix C. Common Policies, Procedures and Guidelines for Managing Information Security). Security policies should be supported at the highest level of the business.

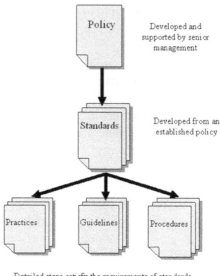

Figure 12. Outputs from a Policy

Security policies should become living documents that are updated, distributed, and read regularly by all employees, contractors, and select suppliers. Policies are developed and sanctioned by senior management and are used as the foundation for standards adopted by an organization. Policies and standards are used to develop practices that incorporate detailed steps that when followed will satisfy the requirements of an organization's standards and policies. The standards that are developed from policies are used in creating the practices, guidelines, and procedures used to support the information security policy framework as defined in Figure 12.

An information security policy framework consists of the following:

1. Purpose (including goals, risks, and auditing)

2. Scope (covers the who, what, where, when, why, how)

3. Physical security (locks, backups, classification, retention)

4. User education on information security (roles, responsibilities, authentication, e-mail, viruses)

5. Security administration (account and rights management)

6. Application and database security (engineering and design, development, production, accounting, monitoring)

7. Operating system (OS) and the network operating system (NOS) administrator practices

8. Network security (all client-server systems and network electronics)

9. Security enforcement (logging, reporting, enforcement, and management, including failure to comply)

10. Support (help desk, desktop support, security desk, information library, escalation)[36]

Figure 13. Information Security Policy Framework

Any training and awareness program should address communications at all levels of an organization and all aspects of information security (see Figure 13). This segment of the information security program should be continuous, pervasive, and an integral part of the overall training curriculum for employees, contractors, and select vendors. The program should offer bidirectional communications—information that is passed down through the organization from senior leadership as well as senior leadership's soliciting user feedback. This segment of the program is designed around the security architecture and technical security standards.

The security management structure should offer a centralized and decentralized resource deployment to provide coverage for all departments in all locations. This approach enables a rapid response and development and integration of people, processes, and technologies. Roles and responsibilities should be cross-functional because security is everyone's responsibility. The security management structure takes into consideration the state of security by performing a gap analysis. The gap analysis focuses on where the major threats and vulnerabilities exist, comparing the organization's security posture to published standards, best practices, and peers, and on how to obtain the greatest returns for the money spent on security.

The gap analysis includes conducting detailed security audits. Questions that should be asked include the following:

1. What security threats and interruptions are considered a vulnerability or exposure?

2. Is the organization able to respond timely to security incidents?

3. How will the organization know that it is under attack or has been exposed to an attack?

4. Is the organization receiving value for the money spent on security?

5. Are there any costs or efficiency opportunities internal or external to the organization?

6. Is a security assessment an integral part of any new business and technology initiatives?

7. If the company is an Internet-based business or a business with a Web site, have the security ramifications been considered?

8. Does the current security infrastructure (i.e., organization, process, policy, technology) satisfy the business strategy and requirements?

9. How does the organization compare to its industry and peers?

Asking these questions will lead to an objective and comprehensive assessment of the security posture for the organization. The results will provide an overview of security effectiveness and the associated links to technology and business initiatives. The results will also provide an understanding of the major risks, issues, and to some extent root causes.

Moving the program beyond documentation, the administration and maintenance of processes need to address enforcement, monitoring, correct response and when needed, recovery. At a minimum, an annual review of the established information security program is recommended to identify and document lessons learned and incorporate these lessons into the continuous improvement process.

Best practices suggest that an appropriate corporate governance framework and methodologies are needed. Three corporate governance frameworks—ISO, Control Objectives for Information and Related Technology (CobiT), and

Carnegie Mellon Software Engineering Institute (SEI) Capability Maturity Model (CMM)—serve as great starting points and as benchmarks for organizations around the world. The *ISO 9000* series is composed of a number of standards focused on quality through common procedures. *CobiT* is a set of best practices for IT management having four primary stages—plan and organize, acquire and implement, deliver and support, and monitor and evaluate. *CMM* is a collection of instructions designed to provide better control over the software development process through five levels of maturity—initial, repeatable, defined, managed, and optimized.

These are frameworks for risk management and information security that are recognized internationally and universally applied across an IT organization. Using one or more of the three frameworks suggested will provide a solid foundation for building a risk management program focused on information security. These frameworks can be tailored to address specific needs and used to train security auditors and develop subject matter experts. These frameworks, based on best practices, are proven methodologies of standards, tools, and follow-up planning that are universally accepted.

Preparing for a security audit and managing any remediation efforts benefit from a well thought out project plan. Most organizations require a diagnostic review of their security posture before conducting their first security audit to satisfy insurance carriers' base requirements, regulatory compliance such as that required by SOX, or industry standards as outlined by the Payment Card Industry (PCI), for example. Many of the requirements are universal and needed for each program, and others are unique. Building a project plan that takes the relationships and concerns of each into consideration is key to an efficient and cost-effective information security program. Information security projects typically necessitate client and vendor involvement and working with constrained resources. The combination of these factors makes the control and management of the project more difficult.

An information security plan that uses a consistent approach should include the following:

1. Financial system report using an independent auditor who will cite any material weaknesses

2. Certification and accreditation for security and information assurance before installation and use

3. Penetration testing on an ongoing, cyclical basis for vulnerability assessments on all systems

4. Patch management to ensure installation on a real-time basis after testing

5. Remediation of weaknesses identified in vulnerability assessments and penetration tests

6. Systems authorization in a timely and efficient manner using certification and accreditation

7. Critical asset prioritization and protection methodologies

8. Training and education of employees at all levels of the organization and vendors and contractors that use the systems

9. Integration of security into capital, operational, and technology planning

10. Communication plan to include the review of policies, procedures, and guidelines on a regular basis and communicate up through the organization the needs for an effective information security program, and

11. A review of actual progress to planned progress, costs, and resource requirements.

The CobiT framework has five levels of recognition and one level for a non-existent program, which may be used to measure progress of an information security program. CobiT, created by the Information Systems Audit and Control Association (ISACA) and the IT Governance Institute (ITGI), is a framework, or best practices, for information technology management incorporating IT governance and control for use within an organization. The lowest level is 0, "unaware or nonexistent," and the highest level, 5, is when a program is considered optimized. Table 11 provides a brief explanation of the CobiT Capability Maturity Model (CMM) scale.

Table 11. CobiT CMM Scale

Level	Title	Description
0	Unaware/Nonexistent	Staff operate using antiquated processes that do not take into consideration risks and issues associated with the business.
1	Ad hoc	Processes are performed on an individual basis and risks depend on the dedication and insight of specific staff.
2	Repeatable	Processes are routinely performed in a similar fashion by multiple staff members.
3	Documented	Repeatable processes are defined and documented and staff is trained.

Level	Title	Description
4	Managed	Documented processes and policies have accountability to specific metrics that are routinely measured and reported.
5	Optimized	Management reviews reports and makes consistent program adjustments.

Source: "COBIT Frequently Asked Questions," http://www.isaca.org/ (accessed November 1, 2007).

In summary, a risk management program should prepare an organization for new types of security challenges on a regular basis. The information security plan should include a procedure for determining who can access systems while preventing unauthorized access. Security audits determine where major concerns exist, what the specific issues are, and how risks can be mitigated. The security audits serve a critical role in the evaluation of compliance and in making recommendations of measures to help ensure compliance. Senior management must understand that it is becoming more challenging to provide adequate security and perform adequate security audits.

Network Segmentation

The strategy for network segmentation provides for network flexibility while focused on defending against cyberattacks. Network segmentation is based on the assumption that all those internal to the organization with access are the "good guys" and everyone external to the organization who wants access are the "bad guys." We have learned that there are good and bad guys both internal and external to the organization who want access to the systems.

Network segmentation is the placement of firewalls and routers between distinct system areas to control the data flow. For example, the public Internet Web server is placed in a different segment from the internal Web server shielding the network from outside attacks. The weakness of this system is the level of protection offered from inside attacks. To minimize the risk, a granular level of internal network segmentation is needed.

Encryption

Encryption is the process of translating information that is in plaintext and making the information unreadable to anyone except those possessing the keys to read the information. Encrypted information is called *ciphertext*; decrypted information is encrypted information that is again readable. Encryption has been used by militaries and governments to facilitate secret communications. Encryption is about protecting the confidentiality of the information. Other techniques are needed to address integrity and availability. Encryption has moved into the commercial realm and is used in protecting many types of information, including wireless systems and ATMs, and to protect against reverse engineering and software piracy.

Certification

To ensure the security and authenticity of electronic documents, digital signatures issued by a licensed certifying authority (CA) are needed. The digital certificates provide information about the user for identification purposes. The digital certificate binds an identity to a public key. Together the public key, name of the person, and the digital signature are used to seal the data. The information can be verified by validating the digital signature. A digital signature certificate is similar to a notary public stamp and signature.

The process begins by sending a certificate-signing request to a CA. Next, the CA will validate the request using its detailed process. Confidence in the certificate is based on the trust held by the CA. If the request is considered genuine, the CA will generate the requested certification, adding its certificate to the new certificate. Certificates bind an end entity for the purpose of nonrepudiation, confidentiality, and integrity in the public key encryption system. The certificate should follow the X.509 specification that governs the certificate format.

Public key certificates enable secure communications between the server and client by ensuring the authenticity of parties communicating over networks. Secure protocols, such as SSH and SFTP, use public key certificates to automatically verify the identity of the remote host. Secure protocols are also used for logging into systems without giving passwords.

Security Leader

Most would assume that the information security leader would focus first on the security infrastructure and applications and then business models and processes. A strong security leader begins with the business model and the requirements of the model, and then builds the security infrastructure and applications to satisfy the requirements. A strong security leader will understand the difference and apply the appropriate balance between operational and strategic technology and promoting strong corporate governance. The information security leader manages the computing and communications infrastructure, ideally through negotiated service-level agreements and measurements. Effective communications using multiple vehicles of communications to all levels of the organization is needed. The communications should be frequent and predictable in delivering both good and bad news in business terms. Security leaders should promote education and continuous improvement throughout the organization to increase security awareness of system users.

Business Continuity

Every organization faces downtimes and unknowns. Plans to increase the likelihood of business continuity are important. Information and physical security to combat cybercrime should become part of an organization's disaster and business continuity plans, with security spending based on the overall threat cybercrime poses. With cybercriminals launching a new generation of attackers, targeting more sites such as social networking and gambling sites, cybercrime is not just an IT risk but also a business risk. Threats extend beyond systems, affecting everything from marketing and government compliance to insurance costs and legal liabilities (see Appendix D. Business Continuity and Key U.S. Regulations Summary). Legal liability may include the directors of the organization, who may be held personally responsible.

The cost of a business continuity plan (BCP) pales in comparison to the costs associated with a disruption of services an organization could experience. The BCP is a subset of an organization's overall risk management program addressing the need for operations in the event of a disaster affecting people, infrastructure, knowledge, information, and communications. Due to the increasing dependence on electronic access by organizations and its susceptibility to disruption from various sources, BCP methodology and standards have tended to originate from IT-related sources. Best practices proponents recognize that business continuity management practices should include all sections of an organization.

The BCP should cover insurance, alternate sites, human resources management, identification and backup of vital records and electronically stored data, operating systems, and applications and the restoration of this information. The BCP should include an emergency contact list, team assignments, roles of teams and members, and a testing and approval process.

The planning process should incorporate the following procedures:

1. Establish a focal point with clear responsibilities for the BCP.
2. Identify and prioritize critical business processes.

3.   Document in the BCP the organization's disaster recovery policies, processes, responsibilities, and measures.

4.   Cover how damages will be assessed.

5.   Clearly define authority levels and circumstances for activation and implementation of the BCP.

6.   Test, review, and update the BCP at least annually.

7.   Include the costs for securing the financial resources needed to implement the BCP.

8.   Consider automation of the preparation and maintenance of the BCP.

9.   Assign responsibility within the organization for periodic reviews of insurance strategies to ensure adequate and current coverage.

10. Ensure insurance policy documents and contact information is readily accessible and current.

11. Maintain a current listing of mission-critical and important records and systems and ensure that this information is backed up regularly and stored offsite.

The BCP should include a disaster recovery plan (DRP) for restoring IT operations, based on prioritization.

Data Backup

Data backup volumes have increased in many organizations to the level that completing the backup process on a regular basis causes business disruption by tying up systems, storage, and network capacity and hogging valuable IT resources. According to a 2006 survey conducted by BridgeHead Software in the United Kingdom and the United States, more than 59% of IT executives stated that the volume of data backup is disrupting or will soon disrupt business operations.[37] There is a need to effectively reduce the pressure on backups by taking the information that is static or seldom accessed and archiving it off primary storage systems.

Detect: Identify Security Concerns

Identifying security threats and risks is more than building stronger firewalls or enhancing existing encryption procedures. It is not about installing software that launches counterattacks, known as "*hackbacks*." Detection activities require investing resources in the creation of a more effective organizational intelligence and counterintelligence capability focused on balancing business operations with needed security such as the detection approaches defined in Table 12.

Table 12. Detection Approaches to Using Technology

Detection Approaches to Using Technology		
	Detection	
Identify Concerns	Intrusion Detection Systems	Managed Security Services
	System & Event Logging and Analysis	Virus Detection

Hackers will reduce detection during future incursions by replacing services with backdoor Trojan horses, creating accounts with full privileges, and installing rootkits. *Rootkits* are a collection of programs giving a hacker a masked intrusion to administrator-level access on a computer or computer network. Hackers can use the full privileges acquired to provide services to other hackers by announcing availability on Internet Relay Chat (IRC), where files have been stored on compromised systems for others to obtain.

Intrusion Detection Systems

IDS are designed to detect undesired computer system manipulations through the Internet in the form of attacks by hackers. Malicious behaviors detected are those that compromise the security and trust of a computer system, malware, such as data-driven attacks on applications, network attacks against vulnerable services, and unauthorized logins and access to sensitive files. IDS have three primary components: an engine, a console, and sensors. The engine records events logged by sensors in a database, and using predefined rules will generate an alert when unwanted behaviors are detected. Sensors capture security events. The console monitors events and alerts and is used to control sensors. There are four types of IDS: application protocol-based, host-based, network, and protocol-based.

An *application protocol-based IDS* monitors and analyzes communications on application-specific protocols and generally sits with a group of servers. A *host-based IDS* identifies and analyzes modifications to files and systems, application logs, and other host activities. A *network IDS* monitors and analyzes network traffic and multiple hosts as an independent platform within a computer environment. A *protocol-based IDS* monitors and analyzes from the front end of a server communication protocol between connected devices. Using any combination of approaches is considered a hybrid approach and is recommended to form a comprehensive view of a computing system.

Managed Security Services

Managed security services cover a broad range of services, including threat detection, monitoring, analysis, remediation, and forensics, for maintaining the health and performance of systems. Services include firewall management; intrusion prevention, log management; identification, tracking, and remediation of network, device, and application vulnerabilities; risk management and policy compliance; and phishing and other e-mail attacks. There are many organizations that provide these services such as Cybertrust and VeriSign.

System and Event Logging and Analysis

Information security requires the ability of information security professional and networking personnel to read, translate, and understand the wide variety of logs generated by the streams of information generated electronically. *Event logs* are the collection, monitoring, analysis, and archiving of events generated by a system, such as from an OS or database. Rules are formulated to filter and interpret an event as an item that should alert administrators or achieve some other objective. The analysis of system and event logs provides an audit log, can reveal undesired patterns of behaviors on systems, and can diagnose problems.

The analysis of system and event logs should capture information such as when an administrator's passwords were changed and an administrative login ID have been used to make changes on a server, for example. Any activities that fall outside of acceptable thresholds should be reviewed by a security administrator to ensure the activity is not an indicator of a potential or current vulnerability (see Appendix E. Logical Security Reports Review Log Template).

Virus Detection

Virus detection software is a system security mechanism to support networked systems. The three primary types of virus detection software are activity monitors, change detectors, and virus scanners. *Activity monitoring virus detection software* is a collection of memory resident programs that monitor for suspicious activities such as a program attempting to go memory resident, scanning for other application files, or attempting to modify its own code. *Change detection virus detection software* scans executable program files on a system before the system is used;

recording the vital statistics of each application, such as a checksum or program file length. *Virus scanner software* searches for virus signature in memory, in application files, and for code in the boot record that is not boot code.

User and Identity Management

Network administrators need to identify each network user and which resources each user is authorized to access. User information may reside in multiple datastores or multiple directories. Building security front-ends to applications is common in larger organizations with hard-coded access policies. This approach can present issues as newer generations of applications are developed and new security requirements have arisen. With many applications and systems, user and identity management systems enable a single user to access all needed applications by using a single sign-on, limiting the number of passwords a user must remember. The identity management solution selected must authenticate users, ensuring they are who they represent themselves to be. The solution should also support advanced authentication devices such as biometrics, smartcards, or other custom security mechanisms. User and identity management systems must also authorize application access to the appropriate users and have the ability to perform complex authorizations against documented user profiles. Where the need for a user and identity management system exists, generally the need for auditing and reporting exists to demonstrate compliance with regulatory and governance requirements.

Virtual Security Office

The virtual security office (VSO) is used to allow a user to change passwords and set challenge questions for resetting passwords if they are forgotten. The virtual security office can also include other tools that support telecommuting that moves work to workers remotely, away from the home office. The VSO may also be used to manage confidential material for an organization, such as sales and customer data, by monitoring the activities of staff on networked attacked devices. The third common use of a VSO is for an online, real-time security monitoring and alert system for crisis management. Such a VSO could provide detection of online system attacks and counterstrike technology.

Response: Respond and Improve

Response approaches are the steps taken when reacting to a possible security breach as outlined in Table 13.

Table 13. Response Approaches to Using Technology

	Response Approaches to Using Technology	
	Response	
Respond and	Real-Time Alerts	Active Resets
Improve	Console Notification	System Analysis Tools
	Restrict Access	Event Investigation Processes/Forensics

Real-Time Alerts and Console Notification

When multiple security devices are deployed to protect systems, these systems can generate a large amount of event data that passed in the form of real-time alerts and console notifications. Event rules are needed when using automated systems that filter the event data generated and specify an action to occur when filter conditions have been satisfied.

Real-time alerts are available from many of the security-related applications deployed within the organization as well as alerts from the vendors used by the organization. For example, an IDS will generate real-time alerts to the security administrator of a possible attack based on the parameters defined within the system. For an antivirus program, the vendor will publish on its Web site new virus definitions that can be automatically pushed through real-time alerts and live updates. There are also a number of government resources that will provide real-time alerts when changes occur to the national threat level. Regardless of the availability of real-time alerts from government agencies, 95% of the critical infrastructure is owned and managed by the private sector.[38]

Console notifications are based on an organization's allowing clients to sign up for its alert services. Console notifications can cover a range of topics, from information on packets with invalid TCP flags, to detection of a network flood, to new viruses and worms and their risk levels.

Restricting Access

Access to computing systems can be restricted at many levels and using multiple methods. Password protection, key cards, PINs, and multifactor authentication methods that include biometrics in the form of fingerprint IDs, face recognition, handprints, and iris recognition can be employed for both physical and network access.

Many consumers rely on software filtering programs to protect their children from unsuitable content on the Internet. The level of usefulness for these filters varies as children quickly learn how to circumvent the parental controls. In the workplace, much information is exchanged through instant messaging (IM) using online services such as Yahoo and MSN. Organizations that fail to block Internet chat rooms and IM services could experience serious consequences as these become vulnerabilities that can be easily attacked by computer hackers, worms, and viruses.

Active Resets

Resets are a method used on computing systems to clear errors or events in an effort to return the system to its normal state in a controlled manner. Resets are common within some software when they time out or an error occurs without resetting or rebooting the hardware. An example of a software active reset is a self-service reset password management application that allows end users to reset their own passwords through an interface that allows for validation of the user, which is secure and easy to use. Validation questions may involve preselected questions and answers, account information, or some other variable that is unique to the end user.

There are times when the operating system communicates with an application. A system may want to talk to the application after a reset. Active reset will notify each application that a reset has occurred, such as when using the Palm OS on a PDA. In design hardware supporting in-system programs, active resets are allowed for the in-system programmer to reset a target system, such as the power supply or PINs associated with the system clock, for example.

Active resets are also used on hardware such as on a module that provides USB connectivity to a PC. Active resets for the memory used by the module may be set to active reset while an application is accessing the module.

System Analysis Tools

There is a host of freeware, shareware, and commercially available system analysis tools focused on system and network security. System analysis tools are used to detect and remove malicious code. Scanning and analysis tools enable security administration to observe what the attacker sees to find system vulnerabilities. The administrator's toolkit includes vulnerability and port scanners, content filters, trap and trace, packet sniffers, and other open source tools.

Event Investigation Processes and Forensics

There are several models used for cybercrime investigations. *Lee's Model of Scientific Crime Scene Investigation* is a systematic and methodical approach for managing the crime scene investigation.[39] Lee's model covers recognition, identification, individualization, and reconstruction. *Recognition* is the identification of items or patterns of what may become potential evidence. *Identification* involves the classification and comparison of the evidence. *Individualization* is the process of evaluating and interpreting whether the evidence gathered is unique to a particular individual or event. *Reconstruction* involves reporting and presenting the outputs from the previous stages of the process regarding events and actions at the crime scene. Reconstruction incorporates any relevant information that was obtained.

The *Casey Model of Investigations* addresses the processing and examination of digital evidence.[40] The process begins with recognition, followed by preservation, collection, and documentation. The next step is the classification, comparison, and individualization of evidence gathered. And the final step is reconstruction. The process is repeated as the digital evidence migrates from the stand-alone computer system, and then to the various layers on the network, such as physical media, to the application and database layers, and the network infrastructure.

A third model, the *Reith, Carr and Gunsch (RCG) Model*[41], was created specifically for technology or cybercrime investigations. There are nine steps outlined in this model:

1. Identification
2. Preparation
3. Approach strategy
4. Preservation
5. Collection
6. Examination
7. Analysis
8. Presentation
9. Returning evidence

An advantage of this model is that it begins by incorporating the best of the Lee and Casey model. Another advantage of the RCG model is that it enables an investigator to tailor the process to the specific type of investigation while leveraging the commonalities possible in procedures and tools.

Computer crime investigations require an ongoing awareness of the need for a methodological investigative process that is followed for each event. The transport and storage of digital evidence is just as important as gathering and examining the evidence. Dissemination of information is a critical link in determining what is presented, and to whom, and how the information is shared among investigators, computer security professionals, law enforcement, and government agencies.

All activities regarding the investigation of an event should be carefully documented. The minimum information to gather is provided in Appendix F: Incident Handling and Analysis Report Template.

Case Study: Computer Crime Investigation

The case study below is a review of an investigative process used to investigation a transnational cybercrime incident. The case study involves a crime that involves four law enforcement agencies from different countries, and a crime that occurred with the perpetrator in one country, the victims in another country, and the computer resources of a third country.

Description of the Investigation

An investigation begins when a major department store in Greece receives an e-mail claiming to have found a vulnerability on the Web site for secure payments. The e-mail offers to provide details of the vulnerability in return for payment. The store's IT security team reviews their logs and discovers that unauthorized access was made to their Web server. Subsequent e-mails follow threatening to disclose the vulnerability to the media, include a link to the Web site, which the perpetrator intended to use to publicize the vulnerability. The IT security team and store management decide to report the incident to the Ministry of Public Security (Greek police), who immediately begin their investigation. During the initial assessment, it was determined that the compromised computer system was located in a different office (Chicago) from the store, and that the source of the e-mails was in Romania. With three countries involved, the U.S. FBI was included in the investigation, along with the Romanian Regional Center for Combating Transborder Crime and the Greek police. After careful examination of the e-mails and computer-generated logs, the team was able to identify a suspect and issue a search warrant to search the suspect's home and workplace. During the search, two computers were seized. Using scanning tools, the investigators recovered copies of all the e-mails and other relevant information, which ultimately led to a successful prosecution of the perpetrator.

The Investigative Model

There are four investigating organizations (three police agencies and the store) involved crossing three jurisdictions (Greece, Chicago, and Romania). This means that there are four overlapping investigations that will require the exchange of information and evidence.

Identification begins when the store receives the e-mail, reports the incident to authorities, and determines that other agencies should be involved. Preparation begins with the decision to review logs and the e-mail messages on the store's servers. Preparation continues as the need to include other agencies is determined. The approach strategy is to use the evidence obtained to support the issuance of a search warrant for a specific individual's computers at home and work.

The collection and preservation of evidence involves searching the individual's home and workplace, which leads to the seizure of computers, and in preserving the e-mail messages and log files as evidence. The preservation process also includes the activities related to transporting the seized computer and e-mails from the store and the perpetrator's computers to the police and storage of the electronic image of the disks, log files, and e-mails by the police. Examination includes the store's examination of its log files and the police's examination of the seized computers, log files, and e-mails. Analysis involves formulating an initial hypothesis to determine the identity of the suspect.

Presentation begins with the store management and IT staff steps taken to make a decision to report the incident to law enforcement, then presenting their evidence to law enforcement, the exchange of information among each of the law enforcement agencies involved, and the presentation of evidence in court. The return of evidence requires controls that address how sensitive data and assets are disseminated or destroyed. If disseminated, the process must formally document and control to whom the evidence is released and ensure that it was returned to the appropriate party and that there is documentation and sign-off that the process was followed and completed successfully.

Bringing It All Together through Project Management

Organizations have learned that protecting assets is more than having a physical security program comprised of law enforcement responding to incidents, security videotapes, and locks. Cybercrimes present new and complex threats and risks that require a cross section of personnel to address. Preventing and reducing the threat of cybercrime requires everyone's participation. New projects are forming every day to identify new types of security sensors for reducing cyber-vulnerabilities on computing systems.

As with any project, an information security project needs a sponsor, someone high in the organization, and a commitment on resources and support for ongoing education and training. The project needs a defined scope, a road map for deliverables, and documented roles and responsibilities. The project should incorporate a common language for communication relative to project phases, tracking, and reporting.

Information security projects that fail typically have an unclear scope and business need, people begin working before they understand the problem, or there is an uncommitted sponsor or resource. Other factors leading to failure include a team developing unrealistic ideas of how much work is involved, scope creep (undocumented or late requests), and midcourse correction due to a lack of understanding of the project's scope.

To ensure project success, it is important to create a culture of transparency where decisions are based on openly shared information and the decisions made are well supported and explained. Quality should be introduced from the beginning by using good engineering and management practices.

Project management activities go through three critical phases—planning, scheduling, and controlling. Planning involves defining the vision and scope, setting goals and objectives, agreeing on project definitions, evaluating resources, preparing a work breakdown schedule, and determining team organization. Scheduling incorporates project activities, start and end times, networking, people, money, and materials. Controlling encompasses monitoring of people, costs, quality, and the budget; comparing, revising, and shifting resources; executing; and checking outputs. For each phase, a list of all risks that threaten a project, along with a plan to mitigate some or all of those risks, is needed.

The project plan should include estimates and a project schedule. The estimate should cover the effort required for each task in the work breakdown structure (WBS). The WBS assumes an outline format such as that shown in Table 14.

Table 14. Work-Breakdown Structure

Work Breakdown Structure (WBS)	Description
1.	Project Name
1.1.	Activities in the project
1.1.1.	Tasks in the activities
1.1.1.1.n.	Subtasks

The project schedule incorporates the assignment of resources and the calendar time required for each task. The project plan documents relationships and dependencies, encourages setting realistic time and cost estimates, and helps in making better use of resources by identifying critical bottlenecks.

There are many methods used to present the project schedule. The Gantt chart (see Figure 12) is the most popular because it is easy to read and interpret. The Gantt chart shows duration, tasks, dependencies, and milestones using different shapes. In Figure 14, the duration or summary of activities is denoted with a black bar, tasks are denoted with a blue bar, dependencies are denoted with blue arrows, and milestones are denoted with a black diamond.

WBS	Task Name	Duration	Start	Finish	Week 1 S S M T W T F S
1	⊟ Information Security	3 days	11/5/2007	11/7/2007	
1.1	⊟ Plan	1 day	11/5/2007	11/5/2007	
1.1.1	⊟ Identify needs	1 day	11/5/2007	11/5/2007	
1.1.1.1	Review resources	1 day	11/5/2007	11/5/2007	
1.2	Design	1 day	11/5/2007	11/5/2007	
1.3	Develop	1 day	11/6/2007	11/6/2007	
1.4	Execute	1 day	11/7/2007	11/7/2007	
1.5	Evaluate	0 days	11/5/2007	11/5/2007	◆ 11/5

Figure 14. Sample Gantt Chart

Project control includes change management. *Change management* is a method for implementing changes that are reviewed and approved to prevent unnecessary or unplanned costs that could derail the project. Change control involves an agreement between the owner of the request and the project team. This group, usually referred to as the *change control board* (CCB), will evaluate the impact of a change and approve the change before implementation. The CCB approves or denies all changes within scope. The board also has the right to stop or request to back out of changes not submitted to it yet within its scope. The project plan is then adjusted to incorporate approved changes.

When the project execution phase is complete, a postmortem or lessons-learned session is recommended. In this session, an account of the project team's experience and feedback from users and stakeholders offer great value. With this information thoroughly documented, it may be used in future projects as part of the continuous improvement process by highlighting the successes and identifying problems that should be addressed in future projects or phases of a project.

Building the Human Firewall

"A Human Firewall is defined as a comprehensive approach recognizing that information security critically depends on people in order to be effective. The Human Firewall acknowledges that every worker who encounters sensitive, valuable and con-

fidential information must participate as a team to make information security more effective. Clearly, information security has to be improved upon if we are to properly protect the valuable information assets that drive our economy."—Michael E. Whitman[42]

IT changes at a revolutionary pace with the introduction of new solutions and products occurring so rapidly; so much so that a single individual would find it difficult to stay abreast of trends in all aspects of IT. These rapid changes have resulted in individuals and businesses specializing in a specific area or areas of IT. The growing number of specialties has led to an increase in the number of education and training programs available.

Education and Training

Education is a critical component in reducing the likelihood of becoming a victim of cybercrime. Education should be for all, including all who log onto an organization's network. One form of education is to include Internet safety in the welcome and tutorials on all computers. Children, parents, and employees of educational institutions should be taught Internet safety as a requirement, particularly on social-networking sites such as MySpace, Xanga, and Facebook. These social-networking sites are used by youth for communicating and by criminals to prowl for victims. The State of Virginia offers an excellent example of training for students in K-12 and is the first U.S. state to mandate such training.[43] The training focuses on applying the same rules online as you would for personal security. The rules are basic: do not talk to strangers, do not share personal information, and do not agree to meet someone who approaches you on the Web.

The purpose of information security training is to teach individuals the skills needed to perform their jobs more securely. The training includes teaching people what they should do and how they should (or can) do it. The primary focus of this level of training is awareness and training. Multiple levels of training should be offered, from the basic security practices for the typical end user to more advanced or specialized skills for IT personnel and other superusers.

Information security education is more in-depth than security training and should target security professionals and those whose jobs require expertise in security. Security education is typically beyond the capability of most organization information security awareness and training programs. It should be incorporated into the development plans of employees, encouraging ongoing and increased exposure through professional organizations, formal educational programs offered at colleges, and graduate classes and specialized training programs and certification.

Information security courses and programs should be created in ways that

- involve all critical stakeholders
- create employable students or students who can advance academically
- capitalize on available resources (faculty, classrooms, labs), and
- support local, state, and national program objectives like the U.S. National Strategy to Secure Cyberspace.

Core learning outcomes should provide

- a curriculum based on sound learning outcomes
- a collaborative environment where opposing viewpoints are heard, and
- an environment where students can learn the components of each knowledge area

Employment in the Security Industry

In 2007, the security industry was valued at $100 billion and growing. This makes it a booming market for job seekers and one with great career opportunities. Security management is vital and global, covering fields from healthcare, retail, and banking security to corporate, national, and cyber security. Starting salaries in the security field range from $50,000 to $70,000 in the United States. Most positions require a minimum of an undergraduate degree and some form of professional certification. Specialties are vast, including global terrorism, risk management and loss prevention, legal and ethical issues, and industrial espionage. Employers are seeking security managers with steep knowledge in the industry they will service, a well-rounded education, and possessing the ability to forecast, analyze, and develop complex security solutions.

To maintain currency in the field, security professionals and students should immerse themselves in security-related learning opportunities. Currency can be achieved by attending conferences, subscribing to security-related journals and newsletters, joining and participating in professional organizations, and following select relevant blogs.

There are many colleges and universities offering information security certificates and degree programs. Schools around the world are adding new programs each semester. One should begin a search by visiting local institutions of higher learning or by going online for current information.

CHAPTER 6

IMPLICATIONS AND RECOMMENDATIONS

The challenges presented by cybercrime are directly proportional to the size of the problem. The problem of cyber security will not be resolved by the efforts of a single group, rather the solution demands a unified effort of the entire international community ... There is a a need for all concerned to act swiftly and with determination.—Professor Antonino Zichichi, President, World Federation of Scientists[44]

Implications

If organizations participate in a process that promotes information security, they will develop transformational behaviors to provide greater security for their business. As organizations enhance their information security posture, businesses and consumers across the community will benefit.

Businesses need transformational and principle-centered leaders who can direct evolving IT organizations to migrate towards a more secure IT environment. Such an environment would enable growth, education, and an enhanced virtual security posture. It is crucial that organizations increase their investment in computer security technology and demand technological solutions that are affordable, reliable, and scalable from their vendors. Failure to implement these IT changes, as shown by the study, will result in increased incidents of cybercrime attacks that are more severe in terms of potential economic and noneconomic damages.

Leaders concerned with the sustainability and success of their organizations' computer security infrastructure must find solutions to the challenges of change in the workforce, workplace, and technology. To facilitate this process organizations need support from many stakeholders. Recommendations include the following:

- A global adoption of a more planned approach to information security is necessary.
- Organizations and individuals should learn to understand the behaviors that affect the likelihood of becoming a victim.
- Business leaders and government officials should increase their focus and attention on cybercrime and security.
- Organizations should invest more in their computer security infrastructure.
- Businesses and academia should collaborate with government and law enforcement to develop a mechanism to identify potential emergencies in cyberspace prior to an attack or disruption.
- A pool of subject matter experts on cybercrime from government, industry, and academia should be created.
- Joint public and private programs and institutions are needed to improve early warning and rapid response.
- Personnel and training should be provided to shift, as needed, the support and priorities with associated information security activities and resources.
- Government agencies should authorize and appropriate increased and stable funding for cybersecurity research.
- Government agencies should encourage and support cybertechnology education programs.
- Governments should promote the rapid transfer from laboratories, academia, and industry of research results in technology and product development.
- Industry, government, and academia should facilitate timely commercialization of cybersecurity advances from research laboratories to the marketplace.
- Legislation is needed to encourage global unified reporting regulations and guidelines for cybercrime incidents.
- Legislators should do more to legislate the rules of vulnerability disclosure without exposing an organization to public scrutiny and lost business.

Internal and external cybercriminals exist and pose a serious threat to any organization. Many cybercriminal stereotypes have mushroomed who are capable of completely and permanently modifying and accessing sensitive information. The baseline of cybercrimes is fluxing. This means that information security requires an investment. Investment in new policies, leadership and financing are paramount. This constitutes definitive solutions to the vast majority of information security risks facing our world. It becomes critical to understand the implications of leadership, policy, and financial investments have on cybercrime.

Leadership Implications

Concluded from the many studies conducted on cybercrime are that many organizations characterize cybercrime as a serious threat to their organization. Given the inexorable means that cybercriminals have to attack an organization and the anticipated increase in cybercrime, it is recommended that businesses develop usable models to identify programs based on industry and size to help reduce their vulnerability to cybercrime. Given the relative leadership crisis many organizations face when a cybercrime event occurs and the negative impact on the business, there is a pressing need to investigate further cybercrime's links to economic damages and computer security infrastructure.

Organizational leaders who intend to lead through changing technological contingencies, who face limited funding and support to enhance their computer infrastructure, and who recognize the importance of a sound information security program are advised to continually pursue information on cybercrime. Acquiring new knowledge in technology and information security is important for leaders in IT, where change and reinvention are constant. Benefits to the organization from improved information security, better decision making, greater creativity, and innovation are inherent, but significant costs may be incurred. Organizational leaders who fail to welcome new technology risk higher incidents of cyberattacks. An effective leadership model is transformational leadership in managing the balance between technology costs and benefits and implementing changes necessitated by shifts in technology. Along with the demand for leadership to change in response to revolutions in the marketplace, redefining the structures of IT is equally as important.

Policy Implications

Technology, healthcare, financial industries and government should do more to push for legislation on the rules of vulnerability disclosure, as they do with the disclosure of communicable diseases. The general counsel within an organization will not share information risk data willingly, leaving those who should report outranked by the general counsel, and therefore unable to report incidents of cybercrime. Governments should help organizations find ways to share data about vulnerabilities without exposing themselves to public scrutiny and lost business.

The findings of the Chatam study are also important to academic, law enforcement, and government policy makers who (a) are responsible for their IT infrastructure, (b) petition for provision of IT investment, or (c) develop policies and laws on behalf of their constituents. Current results also implicate benefits to business community members who report incidents of cybercrime. Training and information exchange sessions could help key personnel understand when and under what conditions they should report incidents of cybercrime as well as how much and where to invest in computer security technology. These improvements support law enforcement and policy makers in pursuing cybercriminals. Business leaders and policy makers should collaborate and provide corporate sponsorship in developing and passing new legislation that promotes greater incident reporting. Including law enforcement and academia in this collaborative initiative could serve as a model of desired behaviors demonstrating the benefits of reporting.

From a macro perspective, cybercrime has further implications for policy formulation and implementation. As the framework for examining cybercrime matures, the primary stakeholders in policy creation and allocation of resources to combat cybercrime are law enforcement, the business community, consumers, academia, and government policy makers. It seems imperative that these groups collectively reach the consensus that cybercrime is a major social issue that continues to grow as the world becomes increasingly dependent on computers and the networking of various computing devices. The world has experienced significant events because of computer shortcomings, such as the 2003 power failures on the eastern seaboard of the United States and in London committed by cybercriminals. The disruptions forced emergency centers to operate on generators, many businesses closing their doors including banking institutions and ATMs, mail service disruptions, and implementation of business disaster plans that resulted in the lost of millions of dollars.

To mobilize resources and implement policies that will protect global economies from cybercrimes, businesses should recognize that computer misuse within an organization has the capability to create major social problems. Cybercrime is a major threat to domestic and national security because of the potential impact of these crimes on the economy and critical infrastructures.

The business community generally appears to view cybercrime as becoming a more serious threat to their business as attacks increase in severity and frequency, and as the computer infrastructure increases in complexity. It is likely that when a business is not aware of certain types of cybercrimes, that ignorance may become its greatest threat. Cybercrimes have the ability to cause major damage to any business. Until business leaders, law enforcement, and government policy makers are able to garner sufficient resources and training, true reform in how businesses protect their systems will continue to lag.

Legislation has been enacted around the world to support significant reductions in cybercrime. For instance, the United Kingdom is strengthening the Computer Misuse Act of 1990 to target denial-of-service attacks used to extort online gambling operators. Still, many countries do not currently have special rules to combat cybercrime; instead, they rely on existing rules and legislation and apply them to the criminal conduct committed in cyberspace, such as the Federal Criminal Code used in Mexico. There are advocacy groups who seek to limit government intervention so that individuals can retain a greater level of control over who has access to information about them, whereas victims of cybercrime often want the business community and government to do more.

Despite the best efforts of many governments, without adequate funding for law enforcement, progress is limited. Experts agree that it will take a monumental event to provide the government funding necessary to realize the true scope of the benefits that could be realized from new regulations. Likewise, cost considerations for businesses are important, particularly for small businesses. Compliance with HIPAA, GLBA, and Sarbanes-Oxley (SOX) in the United States, for example, coupled with required security measures to prevent identity theft, could literally bankrupt a business, or position their pricing model so that it is no longer competitive.

Financial Implications

Given the available resources and budgetary constraints, many businesses continue to underfund, are unfamiliar with, or are ill-prepared to protect, investigate, and enforce sound computer security practices to help in minimizing the financial risks associated with cybercrime.

Economic and Noneconomic Damages

Organized attacks by hacker teams having members with expertise in business functions and processes and rudimentary access and coding expertise are now common. Organized attacks can have a huge impact on a nation's economy, with several major systems at risk from cybercrime, including corporations, utilities, transportation, financial, defense, government, space, telecommunications, and academic systems. Coordinated attacks on any of these systems could potentially cause billions of dollars in damage and would have a significant impact on the economic well-being of a country.

The scope of economic damages resulting from cybercrime should not be limited to actual computer outage and employees being unable to perform their tasks. The economic damages caused by cybercrime ought to be assessed in broad terms because even the impact of a single incident may have perpetual ramifications. The economic harm from a single cybercrime incident can be staggering. Understanding the economic damage of a single cybercrime incident is important when assessing the risk of a cybercrime incident on an organization. For example, in 2002, Hurricane Andrew caused approximately $25 billion dollars worth of damage, whereas the Love Bug virus cost computer users globally $6.7 billion in damages in the first five days and as much as $15 billion during the reporting period. Remarkably, a single university student in the Philippines caused the Love Bug, using inexpensive computer equipment.

Economic damages include the loss of intellectual property, financial fraud, damage to reputation, third-party liability, and opportunity costs (e.g., lost sales, lower productivity). Understanding the potential damage cybercrime may have on a business will help information security personnel and business leaders in making better decisions regarding their security posture.

The economic damages resulting from a cybercrime incident indicate that all types of businesses are vulnerable to economic harm if a cybercrime incident should occur to their organization. Opposing viewpoints and perspectives were noted where the actual costs versus the estimated costs of an incident differed. Because some organizations have yet to experience any sizeable losses due to cybercrime, they consider security for sensitive data on computer systems a low priority. Conversely, some organizations that have experienced economic losses are more inclined to spend the money necessary to prevent future incidents of cybercrime.

Insurance

The insurance industry will be the engine that drives security technology. Organizations that have taken the additional measures to secure their environment may be eligible for insurance discounts that will eventually make one Web server a better buy than another. Software vendors will be forced to fix the holes in their products in order to benefit from lower premiums. Organizations will need to provide adequate virtual security within their work areas.

Return on security investment (ROSI) is one factor in justifying the cost of security. Another factor is loss determination for insurance purposes. ROSI and loss determination can be used in determining what is reported to law enforcement and when to file an insurance claim. A forensics investigator also needs to consider the loss estimates for a case.

Loss classifications used for remediable activities include the following:

- Verification costs to check systems (diagnostic and remediation technologies)
- Restoration costs to place systems back online (testing)
- Market value or replacement value of the property destroyed or services lost
- Lost profits
- Reasonable value of loss caused by "unavailability"
- Investigation costs
- Past and future losses
- Injury suffered
- Loss of computer time (lost productivity)
- Cost of replacing lost data

For example, when a hacker attack shuts down an organization's system, the value of the cyberattack includes the wages of employees who experience the loss of services, those used in developing the asset, those involved in diagnosis, restoration, and testing the systems, and the cost of lost or modified data.

Insurers write contracts providing coverage from cyberattacks that covers damages from a cyberattack for losses specifically described in the contract. Intangible losses are difficult to recover through insurance. Coverage typically includes the loss of all destroyed data, text, images, sounds, collections, and compilations, and intellectual property such as computer programs and coding. Traditional property damage policies are intended to cover only tangible property. The insured should understand the method used by the insurance carrier to calculate the loss in each instance for which coverage is provided.

Premiums can cost $20,000 to $40,000 annually for base coverage. These premiums can also include coverage for first- and third-party liability coverage of up to $50 million each. First-party liability coverage is for direct damage to the insured party from a cyberattack. Third-party liability provides for coverage from negligent acts of the insured, such as when the insured party's computers are used to launch an attack against a primary target unknowingly. Other negligent acts include errors, libel, slander, invasion of privacy, plagiarism, infringement of a copyright, weak security on a company Web server that results in losses to a third-party, megatags with another company's names on its Web pages, or the negligent provision of professional services.

Before providing cyberattack coverage, the insurance company will conduct a security audit or survey of the client's site to determine the level of insurance risks. The security assessment firm can provide a thorough due diligence security audit of the network before the insurance company considers issuing a policy. The insured should thoroughly review and understand the income losses and revenue losses from an attack that are covered.

To compare the cost of insurance to what a single incident would cost a method to determine the unavailability loss is as follows:

> *The annual sales for an organization are scheduled to increase between 15% and 20%, an average increase of 17.5%. With sales of $14 million in 2006, a 17.5% increase equates to $16,450,000 ($14,000,000 x 1.175). When the Web site of the organization is disabled for one day, the cost of the loss is $6,712.*

$$\$16,450,000 - \$14,000,000 = \$2,450,000$$

$$\$2,450,000/365 \text{ days} = \$6,712$$

This is the tangible cost, excluding employee wages to diagnose, test, and restore the Web page. This price also excludes the costs of the effects of dissatisfied consumers who elect not to return to the site because they could not use it at the desired time.

Recommendations

Do you have multiple door locks and a high-tech security system at your office? It could be that tighter security for your computer system is also what you need.[45]

Legislative

1. A national standard should be created and universally accepted that defines cybercrime and develops a single national database to gather and compile data.

2. Legislation should be established that reduces the risks to businesses when reporting incidents of cybercrime and some level of education should be required that encourages incident reporting.

3. Industry leaders should call for a major overhaul of local, state, and national efforts to deal with cybercrime. There should be a call for a national debate to raise awareness of this issue and who will be responsible for addressing the outcomes of the debates at the highest levels of government.

4. Stronger enforcement of laws relating to electronic crimes is needed.

5. Stronger prosecution of cybercrime, including cybercrime committed in one jurisdiction yet having effects in another, is needed.

6. There is an urgent need to improve the effectiveness and efficiency of tools and actions at the national and the international level to promote international cooperation among law enforcement agencies on cybercrime.

Industry Collaboration

1. Ongoing research is needed to examine the concept of common infrastructures as they relate to cybercrime.

2. More scientific data are needed on victimization and the economic and noneconomic harm victims' experience.

3. Education about cybercrime in emerging economies and regions where computers are less prevalent is needed.

4. Research is needed on significant relationships between business demographics and the level of risks and consequences associated with cybercrime.

Business Practices

1. Businesses and individuals must have the autonomy to conduct business ethically and profitably.

2. Businesses should establish policies, ensuring that people are trained and aware of the policies, and ensuring that technology has been purchased to support the policies.

3. Build a profile on high-risk employees, such as seasonal or temporary workers, or others with access to sensitive data.

4. Call centers are also prime fraud targets. Benchmark what a typical call to the center should look like and then randomly scan the database for calls that do not fit the profile. For example, if a call type typically requires an

analyst to access one file, but several files are accessed, the scan should highlight the discrepancy.

5. Data retention policies should identify what data may be purged from the system, when, and under what conditions.

6. Organizations should create and implement security processes and policies and encourage a culture that is consistent in its focus on improved security.

7. Policies, procedures, and guidelines regarding the infrastructure and applications should cover the big picture, including vulnerabilities, authentication, and closing backdoors in applications and systems.

8. ISP and other network providers or hosts should protect themselves with solid "terms of use" agreements, which should prohibit any illegal activities, including the illegal activities covered under the agreement.

Leadership Practices

1. Organizations should provide sufficient funding for periodic conversion and migration of technology to avoid technological obsolescence and degradation of storage media.

2. Key management activities should include the following:

   a. Create security policies to match the size and culture of your business. Policies must be written, enforced, and kept updated.

   b. Establish a computer software and hardware asset inventory list and create a life cycle plan for each device.

   c. Classify data according to usage and sensitivity. Establish owners of all data assets. Identify data covered by specific regulations and requirements (federal laws, credit card information).

   d. Prepare a comprehensive budget. Ensure that security is a specific budget line item.

3. Managers should meet regularly to exchange information and learn of new ideas.

4. Do not allow users to add hardware or software to computers without proper authorization.

5. Management must recognize that when technology becomes outdated, there is a risk of loss of data integrity to threats and attacks. Prevention

of technology obsolesce requires proper planning by management. When obsolescence is identified, management must take action.

6. The most important thing is to have a consistent security policy and make sure everyone reads it and knows it.

7. The role of CSO or CPO ideally is to be a dedicated resource. At a minimum the role should become a specified part of the job of someone within the organization, such as the lead auditor or network administrator.

8. Ensure that your global security team has ample time to stay current.

9. Provide recognition, education, and tracking to enable all staff to participate in the information security program.

Security Team

1. Keep your ISP's emergency contact number on hand. Do not rely on the regular phone number for billing or use e-mail addresses for critical emergencies.

2. Ask your ISP what kind of technologies it is using to detect and stop floods. If the ISP does not answer appropriately, suggest that the ISP investigate such technologies.

3. Deploy automated sensor networks as a flood-control technology to detect and instantly throttle the traffic patterns associated with denial-of-service floods.

4. Deploy both antivirus and antispyware tools, and keep them updated on a daily basis.

5. Patch system vulnerabilities, especially client-side vulnerabilities in browsers, to reduce deployment of bots.

6. Make sure you rapidly test and apply the latest patches in your environment.

7. Keep software up to date. When vendors release patches for software operating on your network, test and install them as soon as possible.

8. When new vulnerabilities are discovered, for which there is not yet a patch, consider the work-arounds offered by vendors.

Physical Security

1. Screen visitors that come to your place of business. For highly sensitive areas, conduct identification checks against federal and private databases, such as local police, FBI databases and a company database.

2. Use a handheld wireless scanner to gather data from documents, such as U.S. and Canadian driver's licenses, passports, and military or government ID cards, to ensure their validity and that they have not been canceled, stolen, or previously barred from a facility.

3. Do not leave devices unattended in public or easily accessible areas.

4. Initiate a badge program that includes an employee picture, color coded for specific areas. The badge should include a toll free telephone number and a P.O. Box to return if lost. The badge should not include the name of the organization, the physical address, or local telephone number.

5. Lock up portable equipment, such as laptops, memory sticks, and PDAs, out of sight and in a safe storage place when you are away from the desk for extended periods of time.

6. Do not allow the removal of computers or storage media from the work area or facility without ensuring that the person removing them has authorization and a valid reason.

7. Provide locks or cables to prevent theft, and lock computer cases.

8. Make it a policy to question anyone who does not display an ID badge.

9. Ensure that all guests are escorted, observed, and supervised for the duration of their visit.

10. Do not allow anyone, including vendors, to connect their personal computing devices to the company's network.

11. Watch for "tailgaters" or those who "piggyback." These individuals wait for someone with access to enter into a controlled area, and then follow the authorized individual through the door.

12. Place monitors and printers away from windows and areas where unauthorized persons could easily observe them.

13. Shred or otherwise destroy all sensitive information and media when it is no longer necessary.

14. Do not leave documents unattended at fax machines or printers.

Response Planning

1. Forces of nature will occur. To avoid many of these threats, management must implement controls to limit damage and also prepare contingency plans for continued operations.

2. Develop contacts with representatives of major credit card companies, FTC, FBI, and other national and local government agencies that are involved in battling cybercrime so that your organization has the appropriate contacts in the event of an incident (See Appendix G. Helpful Resources).

3. Have an incident response plan that everyone knows and can quickly access in an emergency.

4. The incident response plan should be a bulleted list so people know what to do in case of a security incident. The list should include:

   a. Pull the machine off the network.

   b. Inform both the IT and business owners of the problem.

   c. Clean the machine up and fix whatever is damaged.

   d. Restore the data.

   e. Call the director of public relations, the appropriate department heads to inform them of the incident.

5. Build a business continuity plan (BCP) for your organization. The cost is relatively little in comparison to what an organization could potentially lose in a major incident.

6. Key deliverables of a BCP are as follows:

   a. Publish the disaster recovery plan.

   b. Keep the plan current and review it periodically.

   c. Train participants on the details of the plan.

   d. Store essential resources off-site, preferably at multiple secure locations.

   e. Have a list of equipment, supplies, and documentation needed off-site, including backup tapes or disks.

   f. Conduct a test of the disaster plan annually.

   g. Routine security testing, regularly scheduled self-risk assessments and third-party security audits must be performed.

Passwords

1. Prevent password attacks by using "crack-proof" passwords and stringent security practices.

2. Choose devices that allow you to protect your information with passwords.

3. Do not choose options that allow your computer to remember your passwords.

4. Select passwords that will be difficult for thieves to guess, and use different passwords for different programs and devices. Also adhere to the following:

   a. Require at least eight characters for passwords.

   b. Do not use "real" words found in the dictionary, names of operating systems, names of fictional characters, names of favorite songs, singers, actors, and films. Use a combination of uppercase and lowercase letters, numbers, and special characters.

   c. Do not use any "real" words backward, prepended or appended by a digit.

   d. Use at least three of the four character types. Consider using a mnemonic, such as C&ctyt2bwb: "Cabbage and corn turn yellow then to brown when burned," something that is easy to remember and does not have any vowels.

   e. Do not use any dates (birthdays, anniversaries) or repeated characters.

   f. Change the administrator or root password periodically.

   g. Have users change their passwords regularly, at least every 30 to 90 days.

   h. Educate users not to share their passwords, write them down, or type them when people are watching.

   i. Do not store passwords in your wallet or an unlocked drawer.

   j. Systems should not allow for unlimited attempts at guessing passwords.

   k. Do not use the same password on multiple systems or machines.

   l. Do not give your password to anyone.

End-User Practices

1. Disable remote connectivity when not in use. Some PDAs and phones are equipped with wireless technologies, such as Bluetooth, that can be used to connect to other devices or computers.

2. Encrypt files. Although most devices do not offer you an option to encrypt files, you may have encryption software on your PDA, e-mail system, and computer. If you are storing personal or corporate information, see if you have the option to encrypt the files. By encrypting files, you ensure that unauthorized people cannot view data even if they can physically access it.

3. When you use encryption, it is important to remember your passwords and passphrases; if you forget or lose them, you may lose your data.

4. End users must ensure that security is addressed in detail. Key activities include:

    a. Ensure antivirus software is loaded and active on systems.

    b. Delete without opening e-mail from unknown sources.

    c. Back up data on a regular basis.

    d. Use strong, hard-to-guess passwords.

    e. Use personal firewalls.

    f. Download and apply security patches.

    g. Disconnect from the Internet when not in use.

    h. Check security on a regular basis.

    i. Restrict access to systems to authorized users.

    j. Ensure users know what to do when a system becomes infected.

5. Use antivirus software and keep it current.

6. Activate the antivirus software's auto update feature to ensure system security is current.

7. Encrypt the hard drives of PCs and laptops. Free programs are available that will encrypt hard drives, including Microsoft Windows XP for laptop encryption, and encryption is a feature within Microsoft Vista.

8. Do not open e-mail from unknown sources.

9. Be suspicious of unexpected e-mails that include attachments, whether they are from a known source or not.

10. When in doubt, delete the file and the attachment, and then empty your computer's deleted items file.

11. Do not share access to your computers with strangers.

12. Check your computer operating system (OS) to see if it allows others to access your hard drive. Hard-drive access can open up your computer to infection.

13. Unless you really need the ability to share files, your best bet is to do away with it.

14. Back up your computer data frequently and consider keeping one version off-site.

15. Regularly download and install software patches. Where possible check for automated patching features that do the work for you.

16. Check your security on a regular basis.

17. When you change your clocks for daylight saving time, evaluate your computer security. The programs and operating system on your computer have security settings that you can adjust.

18. Make sure your coworkers know what to do if your computer system becomes infected.

19. Encrypt e-mail containing personal data or other sensitive information.

20. Disable whatever technology is not absolutely needed.

21. Protect your computer from Internet intruders by using firewalls.

22. For computer use at home by youth:

    a. Place the computer in a central location in the home where contents on the display can be seen.

    b. Use the Internet with your children and provide continuous parental supervision.

    c. Teach children to never give out personal information or agree to meet an individual in person that the child met online.

    d. Monitor and oversee all online friends and their chat areas.

    e. Teach your children how to respond to offensive or dangerous communications.

    f. If the child receives an offensive or dangerous communication, such as an offensive e-mail, turn off the monitor and contact law enforcement.

g. Reports any suspicious online stalking or sexual exploitation of a child to law enforcement.

h. Set up your child's Internet account in the parents' name with parents having the primary screen name, controlling passwords, and using blocking and filtering devices.

i. Use parental-control tools provided by your ISP and available for purchase.

j. Never allow your children to e-mail pictures of themselves to strangers.

k. Avoid chat rooms or discussion areas that look provocative, sketchy, or suspicious in any way.

l. Do not open e-mails, files, links, URLs, or Web pages that you receive from people you do not know or trust.

m. Do not give out your password.

n. Be honest about your age.

Technical Support Team Practices

1. System administrator should only log in as the administrator when there is an administrative task to be performed.

2. System administrators should consider "run as" or authenticate briefly to perform administrative tasks.

3. IT staff members' key activities include the following:

    a. Maintain configuration management through security policy implementation and systems hardening.

    b. Maintain patch management on all systems. Follow a regular schedule for applying patches for operating systems, software, and antivirus updates; subscribe to security mailing lists.

    c. Maintain operational management through the reviewing of all log files, ensuring system backups with periodic data restores, and report any known issues or risks.

    d. Perform security testing through annual security audits and penetration scanning.

    e. Ensure physical security of systems and facilities. Limit access to key personnel.

4. For application development, ensure that the development and evaluation process for writing code includes the following:

    a. Thoroughly document the features of the application, including any pre-built modules and precompiled libraries. This documentation should cover any encryption, nonsecure network communications, application configuration, and access control vulnerabilities.

    b. Incorporate a process to validate inputs and outputs to minimize SQL injection, cross-site scripting (XSS), and OS injection vulnerabilities, and use of custom cookies.

    c. Ensure the application is designed to fail gracefully, using error handling and logging for tracing purposes.

    d. Balance the need for improved performance with security by including interface-level checks, and avoid the use of native methods in code development.

    e. Build adequate time into a programmer's schedule and provide adequate training to reduce implementation errors that could lead to unexpected behaviors by the application.

5. Train employees on how to update virus protection software, how to download security patches from software vendors, and how to create a proper password.

6. Keep systems up to date with the most recent software versions.

7. Configure firewalls properly.

8. Designate a person to contact for more information if there is a problem.

9. Subscribe to the Department of Homeland Security National Cyber Alert System to receive free, timely alerts on new threats and learn how to better protect your area of cyberspace.

10. To fight against fast-flux, ISPs and users should probe suspicious nodes and use intrusion detection systems; block TCP port 80 and UDP port 53; block access to mother ship and other controller machines when detected; "blackhole" DNS and BGP route-injection; and monitor DNS.

11. Use data loss prevention (DLP) solutions to protect confidential data and safeguard intellectual property.

12. Any DLP solution selected should comply with local, industry, and national regulations and guidelines.

13. Have IT and security personnel trained and provided with opportunities to stay abreast of new technologies and changes in products and ser-

vices commercially available (See Appendix H. Commercially Available Security Tools).

14. Any DLP appliance selected should include the capability to generate logs and reports for auditing.

15. Require all users to log off or power down workstations at the end of the workday or when away from their desk for extended periods of time.

16. At the start of each shift, review network traffic statistics to build familiarity with normal patterns. The review should include the type of traffic that occurred, the destinations and sources of traffic, and how much.

17. Review antivirus log to assess whether you were hit by a virus and if the antivirus signatures are current.

18. Review IDS and firewall logs in-depth to determine whether someone on the inside is doing something improper and who is attempting to gain access.

19. Review the security logs on the domain servers to determine if there were any system lockouts, especially for those with administrator privileges. Ensure that the lockouts were due to human error rather than part of a breach attempt.

20. Check for new security patches for any software in the organization's baseline of technologies. If the baseline has not yet been determined, then develop one.

21. Prior to installing a new patch, review the release information, test, and then decide when to implement.

22. Verify all current connections on a regular basis going through the firewall, both in and out. Check for anomalies and investigate them, such as outbound FTP or inbound Telnet/SSH sessions. Look for what is not normal.

23. Use multiple firewalls within the network, such as a network-level firewall and application-level firewalls.

24. Deploy vulnerability-assessment software to show where the major potential holes exist.

25. Deploy intrusion-detection systems that determine actual hacker activity. (The downside of this kind of technology is that it can have a fair number of false positives.)

26. Use a layered defense in your approach to information security.

27. Prevent attacks by maximizing computer uptime and implementing a change control process.

28. Install a surge protector on computer devices (if it is not a part of the UPS) to guard against power spikes and surges.

29. Install a RAID (redundant array of inexpensive disks) solution to guard against hard-disk crashes.

30. Where possible provide staff with a PC that has a backup hot-swappable power supply unit.

31. Make frequent backups and keep the recent ones on hand in case of an operating system or software corruption.

32. Configure redundant systems for applications or services requiring high availability.

33. Consider building fault-tolerant systems for implementing a high-uptime computer configuration.

34. Use data from your local CERT to assist in combating known exploits and targeted threats.

35. Enlist customized products to forewarn you of threats.

36. Prioritize your technology, mapping it to critical systems at critical times.

37. Electronic equipment susceptible to power fluctuations should have controls applied to manage power quality.

38. Use XML tags and descriptors to "wrap" proprietary formats such as Microsoft Word, Excel, and Adobe PDF for electronic record archives.

39. Use technology that monitors for attacks in the traffic flowing over large networks, including sniffing out botnets.

40. Deploy scanning and analysis tools.

41. Use VPNs for secure connections to home systems.

42. Deploy the use of encryption using public keys from a trusted public key repository and keys from a private courier and where appropriate cryptography exists.

43. Use firewall-generation technology:

    a. Packet filtering firewalls: these firewalls examine incoming packet header and selectively filter packets.

    b. Application-layer firewall or proxy server: places the proxy server rather than the Web server exposed to the outside world.

c. Stateful inspection firewall: uses a state table that tracks the states and context of each packet.

d. Dynamic packet-filtering firewall: allows entire sets of one type of packet to enter in response to authorized requests.

e. Screened host firewall system: combines the packet-filtering routers with a separate dedicated firewall as illustrated in Figure 15.

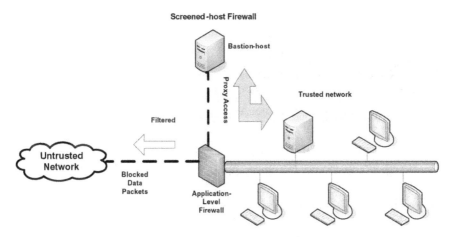

Figure 15. Screened-host Firewall.

Note. Adapted from Kennesaw State University Center for Information Security Education.

f. Dual-homed host firewalls: hosts contain two NICs; one NIC is connected to the external network and the second to the internal network (see Figure 16).

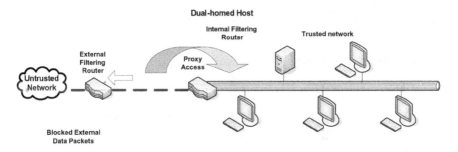

Figure 16. Dual-Homed Host Firewall.

Note. Adapted from Kennesaw State University Center for Information Security Education.

g. Screened subnet firewalls (with DMZ): provide an intermediate area between the trusted network and the untrusted network, known as the *demilitarized zone*, or DMZ (see Figure 17).

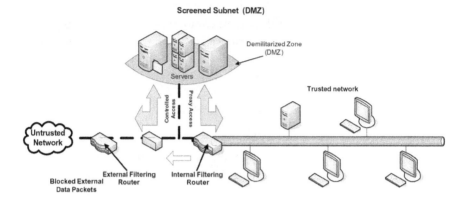

Figure 17. Screened Subnet Firewalls with a Demilitarized Zone (DMZ).

Note. Adapted from Kennesaw State University Center for Information Security Education.

h. Those who use dial-up to access the Internet should enhance security through the use of a remote authentication dial-in user service or terminal access control system, illustrated in Figure 18.

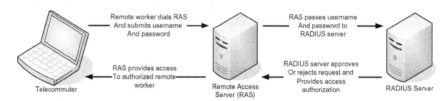

Figure 18. Dial-up Access—RADIUS Configuration.

Note. Adapted from Kennesaw State University Center for Information Security Education.

i. Intrusion detection system (IDS): works like a burglar alarm for a computer system. It can be network-based or host-based and uses signature-based or statistical anomaly-based codes to analyze traffic as depicted in Figure 19.

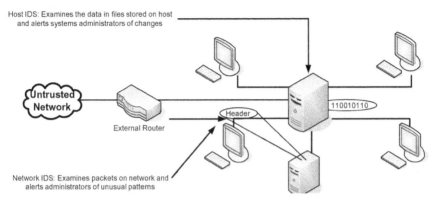

Figure 19. Intrusion Detection Systems (Adapted from Kennesaw State University Center for Information Security Education)

New Technologies and Community Involvement

1. Encourage businesses and government to expand the use of newer kinds of electronic payment systems, such as "digital money" systems, among other more secure methods deployed today.

2. Use a public key infrastructure where certificate authorities authenticate public keys. The certificate authority itself must be reliable, so the certifier may need to be certified.

3. Deploy mobile data cards that double as a laptop security mechanism.

4. To secure e-mail it is recommended that encryption cryptosystems be adopted that inject some degree of security into e-mail.

5. To secure the Web, secure electronic transactions (SET), secure socket layer (SSL), secure hypertext transfer protocol (SHTTP), secure shell (SSH), and IP Security (IPsec) are methods that should be considered.

6. The international community should promote the transfer of technology on mutually agreed terms with a view to assisting developing economies to take advantage of technology in an effort to bridge the digital divide.

7. Improve and reinforce the coordination of activities of international and intergovernmental organizations and other institutions concerned with Internet governance and the exchange of information among them.

8. To counter the growing problem posed by spam, adopt a multipronged approach, including enacting legislation enhanced by consumer and business education, granting law enforcement the necessary authority and

tools, adhering to technical and self-regulatory measures and best practices, and encouraging international cooperation.

9. Set up regional high-speed Internet backbone networks and create national and regional Internet exchange points (IXPs).

10. The security and stability of the Internet must be maintained through Internet governance at all levels of the economy.

CHAPTER 7

CONCLUSION

"Technology alone cannot solve the challenges of Information Security. The way we conduct business now often compromises Information Security. It is time to change the way we think about Information Security—and the way we manage it.... It is essential that we broaden our definition of Information Security to include the people who actually make it happen."—Unknown

Summary

A broad and inclusive focus is necessary to address cybercrime. The focus should include laws, penalties, and law enforcement. The focus should also include requirements for the secure functioning of a cybereconomy, optimizing business confidence and individual privacy, as well as strategies to promote and protect the innovation and wealth-creating potential and opportunities of information and computing technologies, including early warning and response mechanisms in case of cyberattacks.[46]

Fighting cybercrime will require an Enron-like scandal to force legislators to enact and fund legislation to address cybercrime. IT departments are going through more change than ever before. The IT function is becoming less separated from the rest of the company. Line managers and staff are changing from being IT's customers to becoming its co-creators. Technologists are being asked to serve as business process experts, project organizers, and vendor managers, roles that require leadership and interpersonal skills. Outsourcing is carving away large slices of the traditional IT function, forcing IT executives to focus on minimizing the disruptions while getting better results from vendors. These changes will be painful for many IT professionals, but there will be ample opportunities for those who adapt.

The security software market is going through consolidation and change, as major vendors increase R&D, integration, and acquisition efforts. Large-platform vendors such as Microsoft, Cisco, Novell, Oracle, and EMC are entering the market with their own offerings, even as traditional software security specialists such as CA, Checkpoint, IBM, McAfee, RSA, and Symantec step up their efforts.

There is considerable funding and opportunity for innovation, especially as organizations are adopting mobile computing technologies on a massive scale and moving toward zoned network architectures featuring internal perimeters. Security technologies should be deployed in accordance with well-thought-out information security architecture. Technologists should look beyond the confusion to build an effective security control layer and construct comprehensive information security architecture.

There are significant relationships between (a) the percentage of cybercrime incidents detected and the economic damages incurred, (b) the percentage of cybercrime incidents detected and the percentage of cybercrime incidents reported to law enforcement or government agencies, (c) the computer environment and the economic damages incurred, (d) the computer environment and the percentage of cybercrime incidents reported to law enforcement or government agencies, and (e) the investment in computer security technology and the economic damages incurred by businesses. The study on which this book is based did not substantiate any consistently significant quantitative relationships between the investment in computer security technology and the percentage of cybercrime incidents reported by businesses.

The findings suggest that investment in computer security technology and the IT infrastructure of an organization influences the number of cybercrime attacks and the dollar loss that results from a cybercrimes. It is recommended that business leaders reconsider their approach in determining the appropriate level of investment in computer security technology and IT infrastructure. Business leaders should continue to increase their investment to aid in reducing their level of victimization to cybercrime.

Business leaders should be concerned that many organizations are not prepared to protect their organizations from cybercrime attacks. Attention should be given to more adequately secure and reduce the number of "backdoors" that cybercriminals can access. In 2006, many of the businesses reported that they had weak information security controls in place. Concerns regarding cybercrime have grown beyond simple virus attacks and DDoS attacks. Weaknesses in information security are a widespread problem with potentially devastating consequences, such as compromised networks, theft of proprietary information, including personal identifiable information, and intrusions by malicious users. Business leaders, in collaboration with government officials, law enforcement agencies, academia, and consumers, should pursue opportunities to develop a universal standard for cyber-crime analysis and warning capabilities. Victim-friendly reporting mechanisms should also be implemented to encourage reporting of incidents by businesses.

Closing Thoughts

The best cyberdefense is a good offense. History teaches us that a purely defensive posture poses significant risks. If we apply the principle of warfare to the cyberdomain, as we do to sea, air, and land, we realize the defense of the nation is better served by capabilities enabling us to take the fight to our adversaries, when necessary, to deter actions detrimental to our interests.—Marine General James Cartwright, speaking to the U.S. House Armed Services Committee, August 2007

The cybercriminal of yesterday was focused more on self-gain. The cybercriminal of tomorrow will be focused more on causing harm to large segments of the world's population through electronic warfare and compromising key infrastructures. With time, we will reduce our investment on the drug wars since the new war will be in cyberspace.

The infrastructures of most economies are not adequately prepared to defend against the risks posed by cybercrime. Many of the core protocols that run the Internet are fundamentally at risk and have usability issues that encourage end users to make security decisions that are not in their own best interests. Security must be introduced earlier into the life cycle of the technology deployed within an organization or home. Solutions should focus on addressing the root cause of security vulnerabilities in the software and hardware. Changing that scenario is going to require a concerted effort to collect and share data about the types of computer crimes being committed and the people doing it. But it will not be easy.

Cybercrimes, from spam on home users' computers to cyberwarfare on economies, crosses many boundaries and affects various types of organizations and individuals. Any range of cyberattacks take the form of vast numbers of botnets used to launch DDoS attacks by sending forged requests to a computer system that will reply to the requests, with the intention of slowing or causing a system to crash due to the sheer number of requests and volume of data. This can range from overloading an e-mail box of a home user to attacks on a country's infra-structure and online resources, causing significant economic damage. We can expect an increase in cybercrimes as disagreements between parties, businesses, governments, and other organizations occur as a form of harassment that is just short of actual conflict.

In the area of protection levels necessary to safeguard sensitive and private information, organizations must look to the information security consultants and security technology providers for assistance. Some organizations evaluate the initial outlay of costs to design, acquire, and deploy a solution as a purely tactical and costly initiative rather than implement strategic solutions due to high costs. Many of these organizations have yet to experience any sizeable losses due to cybercrime, placing the need for prevention at a low priority. Conversely, organizations that have experienced economic harm, such as financial losses, or serious noneconomic harm, such as damage to their reputation, are willing to spend the money necessary to prevent future occurrences.

Industry will have to remain forever vigilant at protecting control systems from cybercrime. Businesses and consumers need the government, IT, and academia to collaborate and develop advanced security technologies that support a long-term strategic vision of the role that technology should play in the global economy and national defense. Cybercrime will remain an ongoing problem and a factor to manage for years to come. If the government fails to take the lead in addressing long-term cybersecurity, businesses and consumers will most likely continue to make only incremental advances and improvements based on short-term, market-driven, and risk-averse factors.

APPENDIX A

THE RESULTS OF
THE INFORMATION SECURITY
SURVEY OF THE GREATER
HOUSTON AREA

The author conducted a quantitative research study, called the Information Security Survey of the Greater Houston Area and used the data as the foundation for this book. (See Appendix I. Information Security Survey of the Greater Houston Area). The study identified the degree to which computer infrastructures, levels of investment in security technology, and number of cybercrime incidents detected (the independent variables) are related to the percentage of cybercrime incidents reported and the economic damages incurred from cybercrime (the dependent variables). The greater Houston, Texas, area was used as a sample of convenience that can be generalizable to the national average.

In 2002, there were 113,154 businesses in the greater Houston area. Participants in the study included business leaders and information security professionals from a sample of 307 businesses in Fort Bend, Harris, and Montgomery counties of the greater Houston area. These are the three most populous counties of the ten counties that comprise the Houston MSA. Businesses were grouped into five industry sectors as shown in Table 15 and in order of size (number of employees and revenue). The data gathered from the survey provided a snapshot of the most common factors that influence cybercrime among businesses as recorded by the participants (see Appendix J. Frequency Tables).

Table 15. Industry Sectors Used for Profiling Businesses

Industry Sectors Used for Profiling Businesses				
Financial Services	Professional, Information, Communications and Entertainment	Industrial	Consumer Markets	Healthcare and Public Sector
Finance	Professional	Manufacturing	Retail trade	Public
Insurance	Consulting	Energy	Accommodation	administration
Banking	Scientific	Utilities	Food services	Educational
Real estate	Management	Chemical		Health
Rental	Information	Warehousing		Social services
Leasing	Administrative	Wholesale		
	Arts	trade		
	Recreation	Waste		
		management		
		services		
		Construction		
		Agriculture		
		Forestry		
		Fishing		
		Hunting		
		Mining		

Findings

Approximately 45% of the businesses represented had total sales, receipts, and operating revenues of less than $1 million in 2005 (small businesses). Financial services, professional information, and the communications and entertainment industries each represented 23% of the businesses participating in the survey. The businesses varied in size and type. The industries represented were on average equally distributed with the exception of healthcare and the public sector, which had the lowest number of participants.

The top three computer security concerns reported were embezzlement, intrusion or breach of computer systems, and vandalism or sabotage. The top three computer security concerns reflected the thinking of 63% of the businesses reporting. Figure 20 depicts in ranking order all of the variables identified.

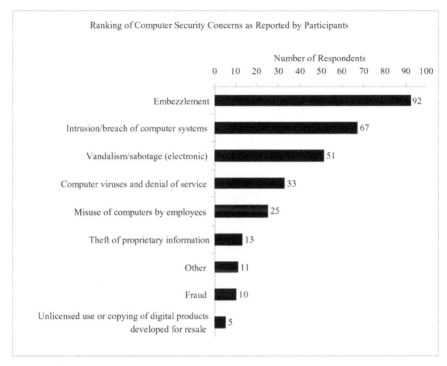

Figure 20. Ranking of Computer Security Concerns

The data indicated that a significant relationship exists between the following variables:

- percentage of cybercrime incidents detected and the dollar value of losses and costs incurred from a cybercrime incident
- cybercrime incidents detected and reported to law enforcement or government agencies
- number of computers, servers, access types to computer systems, and security measures in place (collectively defined as the computer environment) and the dollar value of losses and costs incurred from a cybercrime incident
- computer environment and cybercrime incidents reported
- amount spent on computer security technology and the percentage of the total IT budget spent on computer security technology (collectively referred to as the investment in computer security) and economic damages incurred from a cybercrime incident

There was no significant relationship noted between the investment in computer security technology and cybercrime incidents reported. Cybercrime incidents detected and the dollar value of losses and costs incurred were the most influential independent variables.

Cybercrime Incidents Detected and the Resulting Economic Damages

Nearly 65% of the businesses in the study indicated they had incurred an incident of cybercrime. Businesses are more likely to a report an incident of cybercrime as the economic damages incurred increase. Healthcare, noted to have more security in place than most other industries, had a lower incident of cybercrime incidents. Other industries studied experienced losses and costs from cybercrime equally.

Approximately 10% of businesses reported losses and costs of less than $1,000, and 13% reported losses and costs of $200,000 or more. Another 10% of business indicated they had detected an incident of cybercrime yet did not experience any losses or costs. To a lesser degree, the number of employees and company revenues had some influence on the dollar value of losses and costs incurred. The smaller the organization in terms of revenue or number of employees, the more likely it would detect an incident. Businesses with fewer than 100 employees experienced 36% of the reported losses compared to 6% of businesses with 10,000 or more employees.

It is important for an organization to build the computer infrastructure using a sound information security program to prevent or minimize the impact of cybercrime. Education and investment in current security technology today are the best tools for reducing economic harm. Businesses should use a layered form of security measures to make entry by users with malicious intent more difficult. Manufacturers of hardware and software should build products with security as a core function so that businesses can focus on configuration and education rather than selection of third-party solutions to provide security for their environment.

Cybercrime Incidents Detected and Reported

Nearly two-thirds of businesses reported they had detected an incident of cybercrime. Only 13% reported most or all their cybercrime incidents to law enforcement or government officials. Approximately, 28% who had detected incidents of cybercrime did not report any of them. The analysis found that small businesses were more likely then medium and large businesses to report cybercrime incidents to law enforcement or government agencies. The smaller the business the more likely the business reported an incident to law enforcement. Businesses will usually report an incident if the dollar value of losses and costs exceeds $10,000. Only 3–4% of large businesses reported cybercrime incidents.

The reporting of incidents by industry overall is low with the healthcare and public sector reporting 3% and the financial services industry reporting the national norm of 10%. Businesses and consumers should report all incidents as they occur in order to place pressure on law enforcement to make prevention of cybercrime a priority and allocate sufficient resources to investigate and prosecute perpetrators. Businesses should collaborate with policy makers to develop policies that encourage the reporting of cybercrime incidents and provide stronger sentences for those found guilty. Educating everyone on when and how to report cybercrime incidents is an essential element of the collaborative effort.

The Computer Environment and Economic Damages Incurred

In general, the more computers a business has, the lower the economic damages experienced by a business. Approximately 15% of businesses with 9 or fewer computers had experienced losses and costs associated with cybercrime while 5% of the businesses with 10,000 or more computers had experienced economic damages that resulted from cybercrime. The industry and the number of access types to computer systems, servers, and security measures in place had some influence on the dollar value of losses and costs. In summary, it is the number of computers and the layers of security an organization has in place that have the greatest influence on the damages incurred.

Computer Environment and Cybercrime Incident Reporting

Small businesses were more likely to report an incident of cybercrime to law enforcement or a government agency than medium or large businesses by a ratio of 4 to 1. Nearly 63% of businesses, regardless of size, did not report an incident of cybercrime to law enforcement or a government agency. The factors that most influenced the failure to report were

1. not knowing who to contact or if they should contact,

2. fear of negative publicity, or

3. fear that the competition would take advantage of the vulnerability to gain marketshare.

The healthcare and public sectors were less likely to report incidents of cybercrime than the other industries reviewed. Nearly 10% of businesses in the financial services industry reported incidents of cybercrime to law enforcement compared to 3% of businesses in the healthcare and public sectors. There were small variations for the percentage of reported incidents among the other industries, but they averaged approximately 8%.

Businesses with five or more layers of security or no security measures in place were less likely to report incidents than businesses with one to four layers of security. Businesses with no security measures in place, or just one, are assumed to have a low dependency on the Internet or networked computers. Conversely, businesses with five or more layers of security measures in place were major corporations that have primary market drivers that require a higher level of security, such as credit card companies, or major healthcare institutions, defense, and infrastructure organizations. Businesses with nine or fewer servers were more likely to report incidents of cybercrime than businesses with a greater number of servers. Businesses with 500 or fewer computers were more likely to report an incident than those businesses with a greater number of computers.

Investment in Computer Security Technology and Economic Damages from Cybercrime

Some experts recommend that a business should spend between 5% and 10% of their IT budget on information security, whereas others suggest higher percentages. Despite these recommendations, a significant association between the percentage of the total IT budget spent on computer system security and the dollar value of losses and costs was not found. Size did make a difference. Smaller businesses were more likely to incur losses and costs associated with a cybercrime incident than medium and large businesses. Approximately 29% of businesses with revenues of $1 million or less indicated they had incurred losses and costs associated with cybercrime, compared to 7% of businesses with revenues of $500 million or more.

A difference was noted in the amount spent on computer system security among the businesses studied as follows:

1.   15% of businesses spent $5,000 or less on computer security

2.   19% spent between $5,000 and $49,000

3.   13% spent between $50,000 and $99,000

4.   13% spent between $100,000 and $199,999, and

5.   13% spent more than $200,000 on computer security.

Investment in Computer Security Technology
and Reporting of Cybercrime Incidents

In general, the more a business spent on computer security technology, the more likely it was to report incidents of cybercrime to law enforcement or government officials. Approximately 5% of the businesses that invested $5,000 or less in computer security technology indicated that they had reported incidents of cybercrime; 10% of businesses that invested more than $200,000 in computer security technology indicated that they had reported incidents of cybercrime. There was not a relationship noted between the number of cybercrime incidents reported and the amount spent on computer security technology. There was not a relationship found between the number of cybercrime incidents reported and the percentage of total budget spent on security technology. The research indicates that small businesses were more likely to report incidents of cybercrime than large businesses at a ratio of 6 to 1. There was little difference in the percentage of cybercrime incidents reported among the industries.

APPENDIX B

COMMON RISK MANAGEMENT METHODOLOGIES

Methodologies	Title	Description
ANSI/ASQ Z1.4	Sampling Procedures and Tables for Statistical Inspection	The nongovernment standard on sampling procedures and tables for inspection where by either the unit of product is classified as defective or non-defective, or the number of defects in the unit of product is counted, with respect to a given requirement or set of requirements known as inspection by attributes. It replaced the military standard MIL-STD-105E cancelled February 1995.
APM PRAM	Association of Project Management, Project Risk Analysis and Management, UK	The guidelines are focused on an uncertain event that if such an event should occur, the event will have an effect on achievement of objectives. Risks exist as a consequence of uncertainty. In project management terms risks are those factors that may cause a failure to meet the objectives of a project.
AS 9100 (U.S.); EN9100 (Europe); SJAC 9100 (Far East)	Aerospace industry assessments of suppliers; aerospace standard for quality and reliability	A single standard for use across the global aerospace community to manage processes that focus on quality and continuous improvement within the aerospace organizations and associated suppliers.

Methodologies	Title	Description
BS 6079.3	UK Risk Management Standard	A standard focused on the uncertainty … that can affect the prospects of achieving … goals.
BS 6079-1&2:2000	British Standards, Project Management	A set of standards centered on the combination of the probability … of a defined threat or opportunity and the magnitude of the consequences.
BS 15000-1: 2002; BS 15000-2:2003	British Standards, IT Service management	Specification and code of practice for service management.
CAN/CSA Q850	Canadian Risk Management Guideline	Guidelines that address threats … the potential inability to achieve overall program objectives.
cGMP (Australia, Canada, Europe, U.S.)	FDA Current Good Manufacturing Practices Regulations assessments	A risk based approach to help reduce the number of preapproval inspections for products ranging from technology to pharmaceuticals.
CIRIA	Construction Industry Research and Information Association providing performance improvement products and services in the construction and related industries	A member-based research and information organization dedicated to improvements in the construction industry. Addresses threats as a chance of an adverse event.
CMM	Capability Maturity Models including OPM 3, SEI CMM, SCOR, etc.	Enterprise risk management standards covering operational personnel, supply chain operations, software development, etc.
COSO ERM Standard	Committee of Sponsoring Organizations Enterprise Risk Management Integrated Framework	Enterprise risk management standards focused on improving the quality of financial reporting through business ethics, effective internal controls, and corporate governance.

Methodologies	Title	Description
FDA HACCP	Hazard Analysis and Critical Control Point (audits for food safety)	A safety program focused on preventing hazards that could cause food-borne illnesses by applying science-based controls from raw material to finished products. Better government oversight through better recordkeeping.
FISMA	Federal Information Security Management Act	Bolster computer and network security within the U.S. federal government and affiliated parties such as government contractors through annual audits.
FRCP	Federal Rules of Civil Procedures (e-Discovery)	Governs U.S. district courts civil suits so that they are administered to secure the just, speedy, and inexpensive determination of every action.
FTC	Federal Trade Commission (protection of personal information)	Responsible for educating and protecting consumers from fraudulent or deceptive claims that mislead consumers, and from harmful business practices that undermine the competitive process including the use of consumer information, medical and financial information, the collection and use of information about children.
Homeland Security	U.S. Department of Homeland Security. Every federal agency is developing directives for specific assurance assessments	Owner of the U.S. National Infrastructure Protection Plan providing a broad framework for protecting critical infrastructure and key assets ranging from the power grid to computer systems.
ICE RAMP	U.S. Immigration and Customs Enforcement	Investigate the movement of people and goods that violate immigration and customs laws and threaten national security; and responsible for policing, securing, and ensuring a safe environment for federal agencies to conduct their businesses; responsible for the collection, analysis and dissemination of intelligence data for ICE and DHS.

Methodologies	Title	Description
BS7799-2:2002	British Standard— Information Security Management System	A set of requirements for ISMS that helps to manage and minimize the risks associated with business information. It is a specification with guidance for use for information security management.
BS8444-3	British Standard— Risk Assessment for Technological Systems	A risk management methodology providing a guide to risk analysis of technological systems covering systems analysis, systemology, hazards, probability theory, estimation, defects, and logic diagrams.
CAN/CSA-CEI/IEC 300-3-9:1997 (R2006) = BS8444	Canadian Standards, Canadian Standards Association	An international standard providing a generic framework for the identification, analysis, assessment, treatment, and monitoring of risk.
IEC 60300-3	International Electrotechnical Commission Dependability Management	A general overview of common dependability analysis techniques.
IEC 62198:2001	Dependability. Project risk management for any project with a technical content	Provides an introduction to project risk management and factors that influence the outcomes. Sub-processes include establishing the context, risk identification, assessment, and treatment, review and monitoring, communications, and a review of lessons learned.
IEC/ANSI/ASQ D60114	Reliability Growth, Statistical Test and Estimation Methods	Focus on improved data and data availability in the collection and use of gas and hazardous liquid pipeline data including providing the capability to perform sound incident trend analysis and evaluations of pipeline operator performance using normalized accident data.

Methodologies	Title	Description
ISO/IEC 19795	International Organization for Standardization and the International Electrotechnical Commission, Information Technology, Biometric performance testing and reporting	Defines requirements and recommendations on the performance of biometric access control systems and the data collection, testing methodologies, analysis, and reporting specific for technology and scenario evaluations related to biometric systems.
IEEE	Institute of Electrical and Electronics Engineers Reliability standards	Promoting the advancement of technology ranging from aerospace systems, computers and telecommunications to biomedical engineering electric power and consumer electronics. Provides a unified locus for archival research on the contributions and mathematics behind information forensics, information security, surveillance, and systems applications.
IIA Standard	Institute of Internal Auditors Standards for the Professional Practice of Internal Auditing.	Provides the framework for managing an internal audit department and performing value-added internal audit activities, establishes the basis for the evaluation of internal audit performance, foster improved organizational processes and operations, and describes ways of conducting an engagement and communicating results.
IRM	U.S. Department of State, Bureau of Information Resource Management	IRM Plans provide strategies and integrated management frameworks used to support the strategic goals of an organization including the measures of success for these goals. IRM are required by U.S. Congress as legislated in the Clinger-Cohen Act of 1996 (CCA) requiring capital planning and investment control through systematic process and managing risks of IT acquisitions by these agencies.

Methodologies	Title	Description
ISACA CobiT	Information Systems Audit and Control Association Standards for Control Objectives for Information and related Technology	A framework for information technology management providing IT personnel with a set of generally accepted measures, indicators, process and best practices to aid in the benefits derived from IT and develop appropriate IT governance and controls within an organization.
ISO 10006:2003	International Organization for Standardization guidelines for project quality management	An international standard focused on minimizing the impact of potential negative events and to take full advantage of opportunities for improvement within a project.
ISO 10012:2003	International Organization for Standardization Measurement Management Systems	Outlines generic requirements and provides guidance for the management of measurement processes and metrological confirmation of measuring equipment used to support and demonstrate compliance with metrological requirements.
ISO 14000	Environmental Management System (EMS)	Addresses various aspects of environmental management including labeling, performance evaluation, life cycle analysis, communication and auditing.
ISO 19011	Guidelines on Quality and Environmental Management System Auditing	Replaces ISO 10011, Part 1-3, ISO 14010, and ISO14012-6. Provides standards for auditing schemes and optimization of management systems under a model for competitiveness and reduction of risk.
ISO/IEC 17799:2000	International Organization for Standardization assessments for information security	Defines the code of practice for information security management.
ISO 18001	Occupational Health and Safety (OH & S) Management Systems	Provides requirements for occupational health and safety management system, enables organizations to control its OH&S risks and improve performance.

Methodologies	Title	Description
ISO 9000: 2005	Quality Management System (QMS)	A set of standards that provide the fundamentals and vocabulary for quality management systems.
ISO/IEC 20000-1&2:2005	International Organization for Standardization, Information Technology	Specifications and code of practice for information technology service management.
ISO/IEC 27001:2005	Information organization for Standardization, Information Technology	Provides generally accepted framework on protecting the confidentiality, integrity and availability of the information and information systems through design, implement, manage, maintain and enforce information security processes and controls systematically and consistently throughout an organization.
ISO/DGuide73	Draft ISO Guide on Risk Management Vocabulary— Guidelines for use in standards	Combination of the probability of an event and its consequences (consequences can range from positive to negative).
ISO/IEC TR 13335-3:1998; ISO/IEC TR 13335-4:2000	International Organizations of Standards, Guidelines for the Management of IT Security	Provides techniques for the management of IT security and the selection of safeguards for information technology security.
ISO/TR 15801:2004	International Organizations of Standards	Guidelines for electronic documents, electronic imaging, information stored electronically, and recommendations for trustworthiness and reliability.
ITIL	Information Technology XE "IT" Infrastructure Library of procedures and protocols	Provides a framework of concepts and techniques for managing the infrastructure, operations, and development of IT.
Malcolm Baldrige	National Quality Award	Pushed by the Department of Homeland Security to awarding a Malcolm Baldrige type of award for security solutions.

Methodologies	Title	Description
ASME NQA-1	American Society of Mechanical Engineers Nuclear Quality Assurance Program Requirements for Nuclear Facilities with Addenda	This Standard provides requirements and guidelines for the establishment and execution of quality assurance programs during sitting, design, construction, operation and decommissioning of nuclear facilities for safe, reliable, and efficient utilization of nuclear energy, and management and processing of radioactive materials. The Standard focuses on results, the role of the individual and line management in the achievement of quality.
NRC/FERC/ DOE Directives	Nuclear Regulatory Commission/Federal Energy Regulatory Commission/ Department of Energy Directives	NRC has standards focused on regulating nuclear power. FERC is an independent regulatory agency having standards that regulate natural gas, wholesale electrical power and oil transferred through interstate commerce. The DOE develops standard for research and development of new energy technology, the marketing, energy regulations, conservation programs, and nuclear weapons programs. Each set of standards are based on the respective organizations scope.
NS 5814:1991	Federation of Risk Management Association, Norwegian Standard	Requirements for risk analysis, the description and calculation of risks.
NZ/AS 4360	Australian Risk Management Standard	A set of standards focused on the chance of something happening that will have an impact upon objectives.
OGC M_o_R	Office of Government Commerce Management of Risk	OGC works with the public sector to achieve efficiency, value for money, and successful delivery of government projects on behalf of the European Union. These directives provides methods for addressing the uncertainty of outcome (whether positive opportunity or negative threat)

Methodologies	Title	Description
PMI PMBoK	Project Management Institute Project Management Body of Knowledge	Provides guidelines to address an uncertain event or condition that, if it occurs, has a positive or negative effect on a project objective.
SEI CMMI	Software Engineering Institute Capability Maturity Model Integration (SEI CMM)	A set of standards that have generic goals that address whether the in-use process continually achieves its implementation goal based on five levels of process maturity for key process areas (see Table 10).
TS 16949	Quality Systems—automotive production and relevant service Suppliers	A set of requirements, based on the application of ISO 9001 for the automotive supply chain, providing an independent quality system registration scheme and efficiencies through communizing system requirements across manufacturers.
UK MoD/DPA (2002)	United Kingdom Ministry of Defense, Defense Procurement Agency	Standards to address risks in the procurement process, particularly where a significant uncertain occurrence has the possibility of both negative or positive consequences.
US DoD/DSMC (2000)	United States Department of Defense, Defense Systems Acquisition Management	Provides standards and requirements for the management of iterative processes used in evolutionary acquisitions to meet operational requirements within the DoD.

APPENDIX C

COMMON POLICIES, PROCEDURES, AND GUIDELINES FOR MANAGING INFORMATION SECURITY

List of Policies								
				Regulatory Body				
						PCI		
No.	Policy/Procedure/Guideline	GLB Act (15 USC Sec. 6801-6809) 16 CFR 314	HIPAA §164	SOX	MasterCard SDP*	VISA CISP*	Amex DSS*
1.	Annual Employee Ethics Program (presentation, policy, procedures, training, etc.)	X	X	X	X	X	X
2.	Audit Log Retention Policy	X	X	X	?	X	?
3.	BIOS Lock Policy	X				X	
4.	Business Continuity Plan	X	X	X	X	X	X
5.	Change Control Policy and Procedures	X	X	X	X	X	X
6.	Clean Desk (Workspace Security)		X				
7.	Computing Media Destruction Policy and Procedures	X	X	X		X	

		List of Policies						
			Regulatory Body					
						PCI		
No.	Policy/Procedure/Guideline	GLB Act (15 USC Sec. 6801-6809) 16 CFR 314	HIPAA §164	SOX	MasterCard SDP*	VISA CISP*	Amex DSS*
8.	Computing Security Incident Policy and Procedures	X	X	X	X	X	X
9.	Move, Add, Change, & Delete (MACD process)	X	X	X	X	X	X
10.	Data Ownership, Classification, & Security	X	X	X	X	X	X
11.	Desktop and Mobile Computing Security Policy and Guidelines	X	X	X	X	X	X
12.	e-Commerce Management	X	X	X	X	X	X
13.	e-Discovery Policy and Guidelines						
14.	Email, Internet/Intranet, Voice Mail, & Telephone Usage	X	X	X	X	X	X
15.	End-User Accountability	X	X	X	X	X	X
16.	Information Security and Privacy Policy	X	X	X	X	X	X
17.	Information Security Awareness Program (presentation)		X	X		X	
18.	Logical Security	X	X	X	X	X	X
19.	Multifactor Authentication	X	X	X	X	X	X
20.	Network and Perimeter Security	X	X	X	X	X	X
21.	Network Diagrams	X	X	X	X	X	X
22.	Network Traffic Monitoring and Escalation Process and Procedures	X	X	X	X	X	X
23.	Infrastructure Change Control Policy and Procedures	X	X	X	X	X	X
24.	Online investigation guidelines	X	X	X	X	X	X

						PCI	
No.	**Policy/Procedure/Guideline**	**GLB Act (15 USC Sec. 6801-6809) 16 CFR 314**	**HIPAA §164**	**SOX**	**MasterCard SDP***	**VISA CISP***	**Amex DSS***
25.	Pandemic Plan	X	X	X	X	X	X
26.	Password Rules and Lifecycle	X	X	X	X	X	X
27.	Physical Security and Access	X	X	X	X	X	X
28.	Privacy Policy (HIPAA, U.S. Patriot Act)	X	X			X	
29.	Records Retention Policy and Guidelines	X	X	X	?	X	?
30.	Security Evidence Handling Procedures	X	X	X	X	X	X
31.	Server Build/Configuration Standards		X	X	X	X	X
32.	Software Development Life Cycle (SDLC)	X	X	X	X	X	X
33.	Vulnerability and Threat Management Policy and Process	X	X	X	X	X	X
34.	System Security Policy	X	X	X	X	X	X
	a. Hardware Lifecycle	X	X	X	X	X	X
	b. Software Lifecycle	X	X	X	X	X	X
	c. Physical Considerations—Facility	X	X	X	X	X	X
	d. General Network Architecture	X	X	X	X	X	X
	e. Risk Management and Audit	X	X	X	X	X	X
	f. Acceptable Encryption	X	X	X	X	X	X
	g. DMZ	X	X	X	X	X	X
	h. Firewall Security	X	X	X	X	X	X
	i. Router Security	X	X	X	X	X	X
	j. Server Security	X	X	X	X	X	X
	k. VPN	X	X	X	X	X	X

List of Policies — Regulatory Body

		List of Policies					
			Regulatory Body				
						PCI	
No.		Policy/Procedure/Guideline	GLB Act (15 USC Sec. 6801-6809) 16 CFR 314	HIPAA §164	SOX	MasterCard SDP*	VISA CISP*	Amex DSS*
	l.	Dial-In	X	X	X	X	X	X
	m.	Remote Access	X	X	X	X	X	X
	n.	Wireless Communication	X	X	X	X	X	X
	o.	Telecommunications						
	p.	Account Management	X	X	X	X	X	X
	q.	Acceptable Use	X	X	X	X	X	X
	r.	Electronic Mail						
	s.	Antispam/Antivirus	X	X	X	X	X	X
	t.	IT and Infrastructure Personnel	X	X	X	X	X	X
	u.	Privacy	X	X	X	X	X	X
	v.	Help Desk						

For a copy of a sample policy, procedure, or guideline listed above or consultation on drafting a policy for your organization please e-mail Dr. Chatam at dchatam@ chatamhouse.com.

APPENDIX D

BUSINESS CONTINUITY & KEY U.S. REGULATIONS SUMMARY

COMPLIANCE SUMMARY - CONTINUITY PLANNING			
REGULATION	SUMMARY	COMMENTS	RESOURCE
HEALTHCARE			
Health Insurance Portability and Accountability Act (HIPAA)	HIPAA requires the establishment and implementation of a contingency plan for any organization storing electronically protected health information.	A compliant continuity plan includes a critical analysis of applications and data, a data backup plan, a disaster recovery plan, an emergency mode of operation plan, and testing and revision procedures. The plan should be scalable depending on the needs of the organization and its size.	Code of Federal Regulations, Title 45, Volume 1, 45 CFR 164.308 dated October 1, 2003, U.S. Government Printing Office
BANKING AND FINANCE			
Gramm-Leach-Bliley Act, also known as the Financial Services Modernization Act of 1999 (GLBA)	All financial standards state a need for business continuity. Gramm-Leach-Bliley, FFIEC, and the Sound Practices of Operational Risk call for banks and financial institutions to develop business continuity plans.	**Sound Practices of Operational Risk.** Because a severe event may occur beyond a bank's control, preventing it from fulfilling some of its business obligations, it is important for a bank to have a disaster recovery plan. The bank must take into consideration all possible types of plausible scenarios to which the bank may be vulnerable. Then the bank should identify critical business processes, **including those where there is dependence on external vendors/other third parties** for which rapid resumption of service would be most essential. These institutions should review their disaster recovery and business continuity plans to make sure they are consistent with its current operations and business strategies. The plans should also be tested frequently to ensure that they are executable and effective.	Code of Federal Regulations, Title 16, Volume 1, 16 CFR 314.4, dated January 1, 2003. U.S. Government Printing Office

COMPLIANCE SUMMARY - CONTINUITY PLANNING			
REGULATION	SUMMARY	COMMENTS	RESOURCE
Federal Financial Institution Examination Council (FFIEC) Information Security		Business continuity plans should be created and regularly reviewed as a part of the security process. Risk assessments should consider the changing risks that appear in business continuity scenarios so an appropriate security approach can be established. Staff should be appropriately trained for their security roles, and all security plans related to the implementation of a business continuity plan should be tested.	FFIEC Information Security IT Examination Handbook, July 2006, Page 78 and A-20 (I. Business Continuity - Security)
FFIEC Business Continuity Planning		Defines business continuity planning as "the process whereby financial institutions ensure the maintenance or recovery of operations, including services to customers, when confronted with adverse events such as natural disasters, technological failures, human error, or terrorism. The BCP must be updated whenever business processes change. The BCP should be reviewed for effectiveness and it should take into consideration the potential for wide-area disasters that impact an entire region."	FFIEC Business Continuity Planning IT Examination Handbook, March 2003
FFIEC Operations		BCPs are required to ensure uninterrupted product and service delivery, operations management should develop a business continuity plan (BCP). At a minimum, the plan should allow for implementation of systems robust enough to handle ordinary interruptions to operations and to facilitate prompt restoration without escalating to more drastic and costly disaster recovery procedures.	FFIEC Operations IT Examination Handbook, July 2004, Pages 5 and C-11

COMPLIANCE SUMMARY - CONTINUITY PLANNING			
REGULATION	**SUMMARY**	**COMMENTS**	**RESOURCE**
FFIEC Management			FFIEC Management IT Examination Handbook, June 2004, Pages 9, 10, and 30
CONSUMER FACING			
Payment Card Industry Data Security Standard (PCI DSS)	PCI DSS is a set of security practices established by **American Express, Discover, Japan Central Bank, MasterCard** (replaces Master Card Site Data Protection Program [SDP]), **and VISA** (replaces VISA Cardholder Information Security Program [CISP]) to protect cardholder data. It is an industry-established policy **requiring compliance by all merchants and service providers** that store, process, or transmit cardholder data.	The disaster recovery plan should include a crisis-management team to handle important decisions and training for staff so they know their emergency roles. The plan should be tested at least annually.	Payment Card Industry Data Security Standard, Requirement 12: §12.8 and 12.9
GOVERNMENT			
National Institute of Standards & Technology (NIST) [NIST 800-14 & 26]	"This set of documentation provides a foundation that organizations may reference when conducting multi-organizational business as well as internal business...The foundation begins with general accepted system security principles and continues with common practices that are used in securing IT systems." (p. 1)	The organization's business plan should identify functions and set priorities for them, so that in the event of disaster, the organization can avoid performing least important functions. The prioritizations should be approved by senior management.	Generally Accepted Principles and Practices for Securing Information Technology Systems, September 1996, Page 40
GENERAL STANDARDS			
Control Objectives for Information and related Technology (COBIT)	Refers to an overall business continuity plan; primarily addresses IT continuity planning.	There are seven areas within CobiT to address continuous service: IT Continuity Framework, IT Continuity Plan Strategy and Philosophy, IT Continuity Plan Contents, Minimizing IT Continuity Requirements, Maintaining the IT Continuity Plan, and Testing the IT Continuity Plan.	CobiT Control Objectives, 4th Edition, DS 4. Delivery and Support, Ensure Continuous Service, p. 90 - 92

COMPLIANCE SUMMARY - CONTINUITY PLANNING			
REGULATION	**SUMMARY**	**COMMENTS**	**RESOURCE**
ISO IEC 17799 2005 (ISO 17799 2000 is not obsolete.)	ISO 17799 is a globally recognized information security management standard.		Chapter 14. Business Continuity Management §14.1 Use continuity management to protect your information. ¶14.1.1 Establish a business continuity process for information ¶14.1.2 Identify the events that could interrupt your business ¶14.1.3 Develop and implement your business continuity plans ¶14.1.4 Establish a business continuity planning framework ¶14.1.5 Test and update your business continuity plans

APPENDIX E

LOGICAL SECURITY REPORTS REVIEW LOG TEMPLATE

No.	Date of Report	Date of Review	Location	Name of Reviewer	Reports					Number of Incidents Reported	Number of Incidents Closed	Notes
					Account Management	Audit Policy Changes	Failed Login Attempts	Windows Systems	Event			
1.												
2.												
3.												
4.												
5.												
6.												
7.												
8.												
9.												
10.												
11.												
12.												
13.												
14.												
15.												
16.												
17.												
18.												
19.												
20.												

APPENDIX F

INCIDENT HANDLING AND ANALYSIS REPORT TEMPLATE

Incident Handling and Analysis Report

Date of Report	
Individual Completing this Report	
Incident Report Date	
Incident Closure Date	
Incident Handler	
Individuals Assisting in this Review	
Incident Type	
Security Rating	
Scope of Incident	
Root Cause	
Preparation	
Identification	
Containment	
Eradication	
Recovery	
Lessons Learned	
Areas where appropriate action was taken:	1.
Actions to mitigate future threats and risks	1. Action #1. [Owner]. [Target Completion Date] 2. Action #2. [Owner]. [Target Completion Date] 3. Action #*n*. [Owner]. [Target Completion Date]

APPENDIX G

HELPFUL RESOURCES

- **Credit Card:**
    - **American Express** (http://www.americanexpress.com)
    - MasterCard (http://www.mastercard.com)
    - **Payment Card Industry (PCI)** (http://www.pci.org)
    - Visa (http://www.visa.com)
- **Government Resources:**
    - **CERT** (www.cert.org)—Carnegie Mellon think tank that publishes critical security issues
    - **FBI** (http://www.fbi.gov/cyberinvest/cyberhome.htm)—FBI's site for cyber investigations.
    - IC3 (http://www.ic3.gov/)
    - **U.S. Cyber Consequences Unit**—cyber-security checklist (http://www.usccu.us/documents/US-CCU%20Cyber-Security%20 Check%20List%202007.pdf)
    - **National Strategy to Secure Cyberspace** (http://csrc.nist.gov/policies/cyberspace_strategy.pdf)
    - NIST Self-Assessment (http://csrc.nist.gov/publications/nistpubs/800-12/handbook.pdf)
    - NSTISSC Documentation (http://www.nstissc.gov/html/library.html)
    - NSA Centers of Excellence Program (http://www.nsa.gov/ia/academia/caeiae.cfm)

- Industry:
    - CISCO (http://www.cisco.com/web/strategy/docs/gov/CyberSecurity_Checklist.pdf)
    - CyberTrust (www.cybertrust.com) provides strategic research on security issues
    - Oracle (http://www.oracle.com/technology/deploy/security/)— Oracle's site for publishing relevant security information
    - Microsoft (www.microsoft.com/security)—Microsoft's site for publishing relevant security information
    - Symantec (www.symantec.com)—Antivirus vendor
    - Course Technology (http://www.course.com)
- Private and Non-Profit Organizations:
    - SANS (www.sans.org)—Security Portal with a wide range of security information
    - Internet Storm Center (http://isc.incidents.org)—Offshoot of SANS which publishes Internet traffic statistics useful in troubleshooting an outage or other incident
    - Fakechecks.org
    - ASIS International (www.asisonline.org)
    - International Association of Professional Security Consultants (www.iapsc.org)
    - American College of Forensic Examiners International (www.acfei.com)
- Local colleges and universities and advisory boards
- Journals and Newsletters
- Blogs: (www.clearancejobsblog.com)

APPENDIX H

COMMERCIALLY AVAILABLE SECURITY TOOLS

Note that the products and vendors listed are not endorsed by the author; rather this serves as a starting point to identify industry recognized tools that are commercially available. The author highly recommends that you evaluate and test any product before purchasing and installing.

Type of Tools	Commonly Known Vendors/Products*
Badge readers	RF Ideas pcProx USB reader; Time America TA620LP Data Collection Terminal (RS485LAN and HID proximity reader)
Certificates	VeriSign; Cybertrust; DigiCert; EnTrust
Change management	Bugzilla; HP Service Center
Cypher locks	Continental Instruments Cypher Locks; WideVine Cypher Locks
Data loss protection	Code Green Networks, Inc. (CI-750, CI-1500); Reconnex
E-mail server attachment scrubbers	PCAuthority; Oracle Email Virus Scrubber
Encryption	CryptIT; PGP; SecureStar;; TrueCrypt
Firewalls	Microsoft Vista; Barracuda Spam Firewall; SonicWALL PRO Series Firewalls
Flood control technology	Arbor Networks; Cisco, Mazu Networks
Hijack prevention of browser's homepage	HijackThis; Spybot Search & Destroy; Ad-Adware; Spyware Blaster
Identity protection	Experian IdentityTruth

Type of Tools	Commonly Known Vendors/Products*
Mixed network authentication protocol	Kerberos, CHAP
Monitor logs, event viewers	Microsoft; Event Alarm 5.x; Cisco
Password aging	UNIX—Solaris; Sun; Linux Security Tools
Password saving and recovery (not recommended)	Password Safe (Free); Advanced Office Password Recovery
PDF checker (HP-UX)	SEAL Systems AG PDF Checker; XiFlow
Pop-up blockers	AdsGone Pop Up Killer; Internet Sweeper; Popup Zero Pro
Privacy software	Privacy Guardian 4.1 for Windows
Realtime sniffer and attack signature analyzer that terminates suspect TCP connections	Realsecure Internet Security System
Registry cleaner	Registry Mechanic 7.0 for Windows; FREE Registry Fix, Version 3.9
Rootkit (Anti)	AVG Anti-Rootkit (Free); IceSword (rootkit scanner) (Free); Hook Explorer (Free)
Screen covers	Invisible Shield
Security administrators tools for analyzing networks	Blue Lance Computer Security Software; SATAN; COPS
Smart card and readers	SCM Microsystem; Actividentity; Genalto; KSI Smart Card Keyboards; SafLink
SNMP v2	AdventNet; Fusion Net
SPAM filters	Barracuda Spam Firewall; Clearswift Gateway Antispam Application; SpamCatcher; MailWasher Free, McAfee Free Scan; Sam Spade; IHate Spam
Spyware, spybot search and destroy	Ad-Aware 2007 (Free); Spybot Search & Destroy (Free); Windows Defender (Free); SpywareGuard v2.2 (Free); CWShreder (Free); CA eTrust PestPatrol Anti-Spyware; Spyware Blaster; Spy Sweeper Trail; Yahoo Toolbar with Anti-Spy; SpyCop v6
SSL	PGP Encryption Platform; DigiCert; VeriSign
Switched backbone	Cisco; 3COM

Type of Tools	Commonly Known Vendors/Products*
Virus, worm, and hacker protection, pup-up windows	Kaspersky Anti-Virus 6; Symantec Norton AntiVirus 2007; BitDefender Antivirus 10; Eset NOD32; TrendMicro AntiVirus and Spyware 2007; Lavasoft Personal Firewall; PC-cillin Internet Security (Shareware); Norton Internet Security 2005; Pop-up Defender; The Cleaner (Shareware)
Web site cookies rejection before they hit the hard drive	Cookie Crusher; Expired Cookies Cleaner

APPENDIX I

INFORMATION SECURITY SURVEY FOR THE GREATER HOUSTON AREA

I. DEMOGRAPHIC INFORMATION ON COMPANY

1. In 2006, what were the total sales, receipts and operating revenue for this company?

    ○ <$1Million   ○ $1–$25 Million   ○ $26–$100 Million

    ○ $100–$500 Million   ○ >$500 Million

2. In 2006, what was the total number of employees?

    ○ 1–99   ○ 100–499   ○ 500–999

    ○ 1,000–4,999   ○ 5,000–9,999   ○ 10,000+

3. In which industry does this business operate under?

    ○ *Financial services* (finance, insurance, banking, real estate, rental, and leasing)

    ○ *Professional information, communications & entertainment* (professional, consulting, scientific, management, information, administrative, arts, and recreation)

    ○ *Industrial markets* (manufacturing, energy, utilities, chemical, warehousing, wholesale trade, waste management services, construction, agriculture, forestry, fishing, hunting, and mining)

    ○ *Consumer markets* (retail trade, food services, and accommodation)

Healthcare and public sector (educational, public administration, health, and social services)

II. OVERALL COMPUTER SECURITY CONCERNS

4. **What is the top computer security concerns for this company?**

    ☐ Embezzlement

    ☐ Theft of Proprietary information

    ☐ Intrusion or breach of computer systems

    ☐ Misuse of computers by employee (Internet, e-mail, etc.)

    ☐ Unlicensed use or copying (piracy) of

    ☐ Fraud

    ☐ Vandalism or sabotage (electronic)

    ☐ Computer viruses & Denial of Service

    ☐ Unlicensed use or copying (piracy) of digital products (software, music, motion pictures, etc.)—developed for resale

III. COMPUTER INFRASTRUCTURE & SECURITY

5. **In 2006, what types of computer networks did this company use?** *Mark (X) for all that applies.*

    ☐ Local area network (LAN)

    ☐ Stand-alone PCs (not on LAN)

    ☐ Mainframe

    ☐ Electronic Data Interchange (EDI)

    ☐ Remote dial-in

    ☐ Wide area network (WAN)

    ☐ Virtual private network (VPN)

    ☐ Internet (including Intranet, Extranet, e-mail)

    ☐ Wireless network (e.g., 802.11)

6. **In 2006, how many servers did this company have?**

    ☐ None   ☐ 1–9   ☐ 10–99

    ☐ 100–199   ☐ 200–499   ☐ 500+

7. In 2006, how many individual PCs, laptops, and workstations did this company have?

⌣ 1–9 ⌣ 10–24 ⌣ 25–99

⌣ 101–499 ⌣ 500–9,999 ⌣ 10,000+

8. In 2006, what types of computer system security technology did this company use? *Mark (X) for all that applies.*

⌐ Anti-virus software	⌐ Biometrics
⌐ Digital certificates	⌐ E-mail logs/filters
⌐ System administrative logs	⌐ Encryption
⌐ Firewall	⌐ Intrusion detection system
⌐ One-time password generators (smartcards, tokens, keys)	⌐ None; no computer security
	⌐ Passwords (changed at regular intervals)

9. In 2006, how much did this company spend on the types of computer system security technology identified in Question 11?

⌣ <$5,000 ⌣ $5,000–$99,999 ⌣ $100,000–$499,999

⌣ $500,000–$999,999 ⌣ >$1,000,000

10. What percentage of this company's total 2006 IT budget did this company spend on the types of computer system security technology identified in Question 11?

⌣ 0–3% ⌣ 4–9% ⌣ 10–14%

⌣ 15–24% ⌣ 25–49% ⌣ 50%+

IV. COMUTER SECURITY INCIDENTS

11. Did this company detect any incidents in which a computer was used to commit embezzlement, fraud, theft of proprietary information, vandalism or sabotage, denial or services and viruses, or other computer security incidents?

⌣ Yes ⌣ No

12. **How many of these incidents were reported to law enforcement or computer incident agencies?**

   ⌣ >10%   ⌣ 10–25%   ⌣ 26–50%

   ⌣ 51–75%   ⌣ 76–100%   ⌣ None

13. **What was the dollar value of the losses and costs incurred in 2006 due to these incidents?**

   ⌣ <$500   ⌣ $500–$999   ⌣ $1,000–$49,999

   ⌣ $50,000–$99,999   ⌣ $100,000–$199,999   ⌣ $200,000+

   ⌣ None

Thank you!

APPENDIX J

FREQUENCY TABLES (*N* = 307)

	Frequency	Cumulative	Percent
Total Sales Receipts & Operating Revenue for Company			
<$1 million	137	44.6	44.6
$1–25 million	78	25.4	70.0
$26–100 million	37	12.1	82.1
$100–500 million	34	11.1	93.2
>$500 million	21	6.8	100.0
Total Number of Employees			
1–99	174	56.7	56.7
100–499	42	13.7	70.4
500–999	35	11.4	81.8
1,000–4,999	25	8.1	89.9
5,000–9,999	13	4.2	94.1
10,000+	18	5.9	100.0
County			
Harris	160	52.1	52.1
Fort Bend	95	30.9	83.1
Montgomery	52	16.9	100.0
Total Number of Employees			
Financial services	71	23.1	23.1
Professional information, communications			
& entertainment	73	23.8	46.9
Industrial markets	67	21.8	68.7

Consumer markets	60	19.5	88.3
Healthcare and public sector	36	11.7	100.0

Top Computer Security Concerns

Embezzlement	92	30.0	30.0
Theft of proprietary information	13	4.2	34.2
Intrusion or breach of computer systems	67	21.8	56.0
Misuse of computers by employees	25	8.1	64.2
Fraud	10	3.3	67.4
Vandalism or sabotage (electronic)	51	16.6	84.0
Computer viruses and denial of service attacks	33	10.7	94.8
Unlicensed use or copying of digital products developed for resale	5	1.6	96.4
Other	11	3.6	100.0
Total	307	100.0	

Type of Computer Network—LAN

Yes	207	67.4	67.4
No	100	32.6	100.0
Total	307	100.0	

Type of Computer Network—Not on LAN (Stand-alone PCs)

Yes	160	52.1	52.1
No	147	47.9	100.0
Total	307	100.0	

Type of Computer Network—Mainframe

Yes	26	8.5	8.5
No	281	91.5	100.0
Total	307	100.0	

Type of Computer Network—Electronic Data Interchange (EDI)

Yes	26	8.5	8.5
No	281	91.5	100.0
Total	307	100.0	

Type of Computer Network—Wide Area Network (WAN)

Yes	102	33.2	33.2
No	205	66.8	100.0
Total	307	100.0	

Type of Computer Network—Virtual Private Network (VPN)
Yes	101	32.9	32.9
No	206	67.1	100.0
Total	307	100.0	

Type of Computer Network—Internet
Yes	144	46.9	46.9
No	163	53.1	100.0
Total	307	100.0	100.0

Type of Computer Network—Wireless Network
Yes	70	22.8	22.8
No	237	77.2	100.0
Total	307	100.0	

Number of servers
None	84	27.4	27.4
1–9	125	40.7	68.1
10–99	54	17.6	85.7
100–100	13	4.2	89.9
200–499	16	5.2	95.1
500+	15	4.9	100.0
Total	307	100.0	

Number of PCs, laptops, and workstations
1–9	73	23.8	23.8
10–24	58	18.9	42.7
25–99	69	22.5	65.1
101–499	62	20.2	85.3
500–9,999	29	9.4	94.8
10,000+	16	5.2	100.0
Total	307	100.0	

Access to networks—LAN/WAN including wireless, remote dial-in
Yes	166	54.1	54.1
No	141	45.9	100.0
Total	307	100.0	

Access to networks—Internet
Yes	157	51.1	51.1
No	150	48.9	100.0
Total	307	100.0	

Access to networks—Internet access not LAN/WAN

Yes	61	19.9	19.9
No	246	80.1	100.0
Total	307	100.0	

Type of security—antivirus software

Yes	295	96.1	96.1
No	12	3.9	100.0
Total	307	100.0	

Type of security—digital certificates

Yes	94	30.6	30.6
No	213	69.4	100.0
Total	307	100.0	

Type of security—system administrative logs

Yes	60	19.5	19.5
No	247	80.5	100.0
Total	307	100.0	

Type of security—firewall

Yes	216	70.4	70.4
No	91	29.6	100.0
Total	307	100.0	

Type of security—one-time password generators

Yes	58	18.9	18.9
No	249	81.1	100.0
Total	307	100.0	

Type of security—biometrics

Yes	68	22.1	22.1
No	239	77.9	100.0
Total	307	100.0	

Type of security—e-mail logs and filters

Yes	30	9.8	9.8
No	277	90.2	100.0
Total	307	100.0	

Type of security—encryption

Yes	30	9.8	9.8
No	277	90.2	100.0
Total	307	100.0	

Type of security—intrusion detection system (IDS)

Yes	96	31.3	31.3
No	211	68.7	100.0
Total	307	100.0	

Type of security—none

Yes	4	1.3	1.3
No	303	98.7	100.0
Total	307	100.0	

Type of security—passwords (changed at regular intervals)

Yes	103	33.6	33.6
No	204	66.4	100.0
Total	307	100.0	

Type of security—other

Yes	11	3.6	3.6
No	296	96.4	100.0
Total	307	100.0	

Amount spent on computer security

<$5,000	83	27.0	27.0
$5,000–49,999	70	22.8	49.8
$50,000–99,999	49	16.0	65.8
$100,000–199,999	55	17.9	83.7
>$200,000	50	16.3	100.0
Total	307	100.0	

Percent of the total budget spent on security

0–3%	169	55.0	55.0
4–9%	71	23.1	78.2
10–14%	24	7.8	86.0
15–24%	21	6.8	92.8
25–49%	13	4.2	97.1
50%+	9	2.9	100.0
Total	307	100.0	

Security incidents detected

Yes	200	65.1	65.1
No	107	34.9	100.0
Total	307	100.0	

Percent of incidents reported

<10%	15	4.9	4.9
10–25%	16	5.2	10.1
26–50%	25	8.1	18.2
51–75%	19	6.2	24.4
76–100%	39	12.7	37.1
None	193	62.9	100.0
Total	307	100.0	

Dollar value of losses and costs

<$500	24	7.8	7.8
$500–999	16	5.2	13.0
$1,000–49,999	59	19.2	32.2
$50,000–99,999	55	17.9	50.2
$100,000–100,000	22	7.2	57.3
$200,000+	47	15.3	72.6
None	84	27.4	100.0
Total	307	100.0	

BIBLIOGRAPHY

1   Internet Crime Complaint Center. 2007. IC3 2006 Internet Crime Report. January 1, 2006–December 31, 2006. http://www.ic3.gov/media/annualreport/2006_IC3Report.pdf (accessed November 1, 2007).

2   FBI. 2007. Cybercrime. http://www.fbi.gov/ (accessed June 18, 2007).

3   U.S. Government Accountability Office. 2007. Cybercrime. Public and private entities face challenges in addressing cyber threats. Report to Congressional Requesters: 16. (Washington, DC: GAO); hereafter cited as *Addressing Cyber Threat*s.

4   Internet Crime Complaint Center. 2007. IC3 2006 Internet Crime Report. January 1, 2006–December 31, 2006. http://www.ic3.gov/media/annualreport/2006_IC3Report.pdf (accessed November 1, 2007).

5   Rantala, Ramona R. 2004. *Cyber-crime against businesses.* United States Department of Justice, Office of Justice Programs, The Bureau of Justice Statistics Technical Report (NCJ 200639). Washington, DC: U.S. DOJ.

6   Potter, Chris, and Beard, Andrew. 2006. DTI information security breaches survey 2006. http://www.pwc.com/extweb/pwcpublications.nsf/ (accessed February 1, 2007).

7   Computer Security Institute. 2006. 2005 CSI-FBI Survey results. http://www.gocsi.com/ (accessed February 3, 2007).

8   Same as Endnotes 3 and 5.

9   Association of Payment Clearing Services 2007. Fraud. The facts 2007. http://www.apacs.org.uk/resources_publications/documents/FraudtheFacts2007.pdf. (accessed November 1, 2007).

10 Department of Energy Office of Electricity Delivery and Energy Reliability. 2005. National SCADA test bed. A summary of control system security standards activities in the energy sector. http://www.oe.energy.gov/

DocumentsandMedia/Control System Security Standards Activities.pdf (accessed October 7, 2007).

11   American Sociological Association. 2007. Edwin Hardin Sutherland image. http://www2.asanet.org/governance/Sutherland.html (accessed November 1, 2007).

12   Cressey, Donald R. 1955. Changing criminals: The application of the Theory of Differential Association. *American Journal of Sociology* 61: 116–120.

13   Clinard, Marshall Barron and Yeager, Peter Cleary. 1980. *Corporate Crime (Law and Society Series)*. New York, NY: The Free Press, a Division of Macmillan Publishing Co., Inc.

14   Same as Endnote #13.

15   United States Department of Justice, CRM. 2006. Former federal computer security specialist pleads guilty to hacking Department of Education computer. 06-106. http://www.cyber-crime.gov/kwakPlea.htm (accessed April 14, 2006).

16   United States Department of Justice. 2007. Office of Public Affairs Press Releases. http://www.usdoj.gov/ (accessed July 8, 2007).

17   Pricewaterhouse Coopers. 2006. PwC's guide to cybercrime. http://dspace.dial.pipex.com/town/square/hn07/pwc_cybercrime.htm (accessed November 2, 2007).

18   Krebs, Brian. 2006. Cyber crime hits the big time in 2006. http://www.washingtonpost.com (accessed September 22, 2007).

19   McMillan, Robert. 2007. Half of convicted ID thieves escape jail. http://www.cio.co.uk/concern/security/news/ (accessed October 25, 2007).

20   McMillan, Robert. 2007. ID thieves have a 50-50 chance of going to prison. http://www.infoworld.com/ (accessed November 1, 2007).

21   Tarun. 2006. Cyber Crime. http://www.legalservicesindia.com/articles/cyber.htm (accessed July 8, 2007).

22   Cantrell, Amanda. 2006. Cybercrime on the rise, survey finds. http://money.cnn.com/ (accessed September 22, 2007).

23   Financial Mirror. 2006. Phishing on the rise in U.S. http://www.financialmirror.com/ (accessed October 1, 2007)

24   Instat-MDR, Jupiter Research, IDC, eds. 2006. IT Facts—Fraud. http://www.itfacts.biz/ (accessed October 23, 2007).

25 Symantec.com. 2007. Symantec Internet Security Threat Report Trends. http://eval.symantec.com/ (accessed October 14, 2007).

26 Garg, Ashish, Curtis, Jeffrey, and Halper, Hilary. 2003. Quantifying the financial impact of IT security breaches. *Information Management and Computer Security, (11)*2, pp. 74–83. Bradford, West Yorkshire, England: Emerald Group Publishing Limited.

27 Cronin, Blaise, and Crawford, Holly. 1999. Information Warfare: Its Application in Military and Civilian Contexts. http://www.indiana.edu/~tisj/readers/full-text/15-4%20cronin.pdf (accessed October 21, 2007).

28 Cronin, Blaise. 2002. Information warfare: Peering inside pandora's postmodern box. http://www.afcea.org.ar/publicaciones/cronin.htm (accessed October 7, 2007).

29 U.S. Department of Justice, U.S. Attorney, Eastern District of New York. 2003. Massive Internet and credit card fraud bilks consumers out of $230 million in bogus "free tours" of adult entertainment websites—Bambino soldier, two executives and five companies indicted. http://www.usdoj.gov/usao/nye/vw/PendingCases/ (accessed October 3, 2007).

30 Parsons, Richard H. 2006. Possible issues for review in criminal appeals. Evidence. http://www.angelfire.com/in4/prose/evidence.htm (accessed September 19, 2007).

31 Denning, D. E. 1999. *War in the age of intelligent machines*. New York: Swerve Press.

32 Erbschloe, Michael. 2000. *Love Bug damage costs rise to 6.7 billion*. http://www.businesseconomic.com/cei/press.index.html (accessed June 1, 2007).

33 Lewis, James A. 2002. *Assessing the Risks of Cyber Terrorism, Cyber War and Other Cyber Threats*. Washington, D.C.: Center for Strategic & International Studies.

34 D'Antoni, Helen. 2005. Security conforms to regulatory compliance. http://www.informationweek.com/ (accessed September 24, 2007).

35 Appel, Ed. 2001. Guide for Preventing and Responding to Information Age Crime by the Joint Council on Information Age Crime. Version 2.6. http://www.jciac.org/docs/theguide.pdf (accessed September 4, 2007).

36 Same as Endnote 17.

37 Ross, Rose and Knowles, Hannah. 2006. UK companies more reluctant than US companies to explore new storage solutions. http://www.bridgeheadsoftware.com/ (accessed August 24, 2007).

38   Gibbons, J. Michael. 2005. The Information Collaboration Imperative. http://media.govtech.net/logos/Unisys_Gibbons.ppt#277 (accessed September 14, 2007).

39   Ciardhuain, Seamus O. 2004. An Extended Model of Cybercrime Investigations. http://www.utica.edu/academic/institutes/ecii/publications/ (accessed October 23, 2007).

40   Same as Endnote 33.

41   Reith, Mark, Carr, Clint, and Gunsch, Gregg. 2005. All Examination of Digital Forensic Models. http://student.iu.hio.no/~s126303/Foredrag.pdf (accessed October 24, 2007).

42   Whitman, Michael E. 2007. Leveraging people to safeguard information resources. http://science.kennesaw.edu/~mwhitman/present/HumanSide-Springfield.pdf (accessed October 7, 2007).

43   Hochberg, Adam. 2007. Back to School: Reading, Writing and Internet Safety. http://www.npr.org/templates/story/ (accessed October 24, 2007).

44   Wegener, Henning, Barletta, William A., Bosch, Olivia, et. al. 2003. ICSC International Centre for Scientific Culture toward a Universal Order of Cyberspace: Managing Threats from Cybercrime to Cyberwar. Document WSIS-03/GENEVA/CONTR/6-E. Cybercrime Incident. Geneva, Switzerland: International Telecommunications Union.

45   Ready.gov. 2007. Improve Cyber Security. http://www.ready.gov/business/protect/cybersecurity.html (accessed November 1, 2007).

46   Golubev, Vladimir. 2005. 6th Workshop on "Measures to combat computer-related crime", United Nations, Computer Crime Research Center. New York, NY: United Nations.

ABOUT THE AUTHOR

Denise Chatam is Dean of Technology and Institutional Research at a Houston area college, and offers consulting services to businesses. Dr. Chatam has more than 20 years of progressive IT leadership in auditing, security, business continuity, global application development, and project management. She is a public speaker on cybercrime prevention programs, implementing and sustaining a comprehensive risk management program, project management tips, tricks, and traps, and market analysis and strategy. Dr. Chatam holds a Doctorate of Business Administration, specializing in information security and cybercrime, a Masters of Science in Engineering Management, Industrial Engineering, and a graduate certificate in project management.

Editor: Robert Griffin, Houston, Texas, (713) 524-1870 (fax), e-mail: rgriffin@wt.net
Cover by: Junior McLean, Junior's Digital Designs, http://junior.mosaicglobe.com

INDEX

978-0-595-48170-5
0-595-48170-1

www.ingramcontent.com/pod-product-compliance
Lightning Source LLC
Chambersburg PA
CBHW051237050326
40689CB00007B/959